DYING TO REALLY LIVE

*Memories of the Afterlife; a Non-Believer
returns to Life after a Surprising Near Death
Experience.*

By Duane F. Smith

In Appreciation

Rob Sclosser; always there when I needed him.
Joan and David Vokac, truly, "The wind beneath my wings
Joe Holley, Cheryl Gribskov, Peggy Hill, Solvieg Lozier,
inspiration to keep on going.
Plus three very patient Editors, Wayne Purdin, JJ,
and Moe Cottle

CONTENTS

Preface

At the age of 41, the Author was given five months to live by a Stanford medical specialist and began putting his affairs in order. Being an agnostic and a non-believer in all things spiritual, all he expected after his death was oblivion. However, when his time came, oblivion wasn't what happened. Here now, in his own words, is his first afterlife encounter.

"There to greet me were my grandfather Amos, along with my favorite dog, Butch, his tail wagging in greeting, both central characters in my Rockwellian childhood. There too, was my favorite uncle, Sidney, and my Aunt Eleanor as well as an old rancher who lived across the river from where I grew up. He always had found work for me, even when he really didn't need it.

To my delight there were the others; entities I had known and loved in other times and other places. Some were from this earthly world while others were from other realms, not of this material universe. All were members of the same ancient Soul Group that had reincarnated together over endless eons."

Later, during, a Life Review, he was asked "*As long as you have a functioning body back on Earth, do you want to get "another one out of the way?*"

Being a non-believer, he certainly hadn't believed in reincarnation, but he knew what he was being asked. Did he want to return to Earth and get "another lifetime" completed and "out of the way"?

His response was an immediate and painful "*Nooooo!*" In no way did he wish to go back to that tired, greedy, war-torn world he had just left. However, after being gently reminded as to why he had gone there to begin with, he realized he had no choice, he would be returning. Then, the moment he had that realization, there was a jolt and he was back in his body, struggling to breathe.

After a time of trying to readjust to his old life in light of where he had just been, the author's life took an unusual turn. Six months after his original near death experience, he was taken back again to the afterlife.

This time, as he separated from his physical body, two of his Soul Guides met him and took him, again, directly to the afterlife. This trip became the first of the five times he was taken back there, each for a different reason, but all for his soul's growth and learning.

Dying to Really Live is the first in a series of books the author wrote, with the help of Frank and Amos, his Soul Guides, about his initial encounters with the Afterlife. The remaining three books of the series is about the other three times he was returned to the Afterlife, and what he was assigned to do on earth in between trips and afterward.

Rob Schlosser
Publisher

Chapter 1

When It All Began

In which I question, is this all there is?

1977 - 1981

In my late thirties, just when everything seemed to be coming up roses in my life, something slipped vaguely off key. It was nothing I could put a finger on at the time, just a shadowy feeling that I had missed a turn along the way. Then, over the next year or so, I slowly entered what St. John of the Cross, a Carmelite of the 16th Century, referred to as "The Dark Night of the Soul." Later, I would realize this was the beginning of a new phase in my life, one that I had chosen lifetimes ago.

At the time, my business and professional life had progressed, nicely. Finally, my wife and I could afford what we thought, were the finer things of life, things for which we had dreamed, worked, and planned. These were things that society had taught us, would bring us happiness.

Early in my life, I had observed people who had lots of money and trappings of a "Good Life," and I had decided I wanted to be rich when I grew up. I assumed that people with boats, cars, airplanes, and all of the life's toys, had to be happy, right? So when I was young, when people asked me what I wanted to be when I grew up, I would always reply, "a millionaire."

Our family consisted of two preteen daughters (around whom our lives revolved), the family dog, and an independent cat. We were happily ensconced in a beautiful old Cape Cod house, our home in the idyllic Shakespeare mecca of Ashland, Oregon. In our garage, were the requisite "his and her" Mercedes. Mine was a sedan, and hers, the 500 SL sports model purchased for her last birthday. Out at the local airport were two airplanes just looking for ways to prove their worth to the family: one was for local flying, and the other for longer distances. With a handy ski area just a few miles outside of town and a sailboat for the lake, we seemingly had it all. I had to be happy, right?

It was icing on the cake that my "other family," the kids from the experimental program I had taught after getting out of the army, were mostly doing well also. The program had been for children who struggled with school and often had challenges at home. For quite a few of the students, our classroom had become somewhat of a surrogate family and many had stayed in touch. Even the most broken of the bunch, a little girl named Teresa, seemed to be on her way to getting her life figured out. As I looked at my life, I seemed to have it all, and what I didn't have was within easy reach.

Early in my life I discovered the power of goal setting, and by my late thirties I had achieved almost all of my life's goals, even the millionaire part, several times over. We had been building bigger houses and taking longer and more extravagant vacations. For several years now, I had felt we were just one step away from happiness; just one more "something" and we'd finally be satisfied and happy, ready to really enjoy life. While we enjoyed some parts of life, we always seemed to be just one step removed from real, lasting happines s. Something was always missing.

Even the last six-week family vacation in Europe, although perfect, still hadn't scratched the itch I always felt. Now, I began to suspect that the next bigger and better "something" wasn't going to do it either, and, of course, it never did. In fact, what made it worse was the growing realization that I really didn't have any idea what real happiness was, or how or where to find it. I had come to realize that happiness was more than the feelings generated by another new boat or bigger, faster airplane or a longer, more extravagant vacation somewhere. When my wife began talking about our next new house needing to be smaller instead of larger, to be perfect, I knew that she too was sensing the same unspoken frustrations and inner itch as was I.

Chapter 2

Given Five Months To Live

*The world is a fine place and I would hate,
very much, to leave it.*

—Ernest Hemingway,
For Whom the Bell Tolls

March 1981

As we began to realize that it would take more than money alone, to bring us the happiness we sought, something went terribly wrong. A medical condition that started out as a minor health annoyance took a turn for the worse. The Doctor who was handling my case called in a doctor from the Stanford Medical Center near San Francisco, California.

After a thorough examination, he was optimistic. He said they were developing a new breakthrough operation for what, until now, had been an untreatable condition. In addition, they were about to do another test case medical procedure, and he felt I might be an excellent candidate for the new procedure. While characterized as major surgery, it could offer significant relief if all went well. And if it didn't work, my prognosis wasn't good anyway. To my wife and I, there was no question as to our decision, for without the surgery, where would I be?

More testing began and I was poked and prodded everywhere, and relieved of bodily fluids I didn't know I had. In spite of what the doctors had initially said, once all the tests were completed, it seemed the prognosis wasn't so bright, after all. The doctors, as a group, felt that my condition had already deteriorated too far to survive the operation. Apparently, my medical situation led to an extreme vulnerability to heart attacks and strokes, and there was a distinct possibility I would die on the operating table.

Even if I were willing to risk the new procedure, no doctor wanted to operate on a man who they felt might die on the operating table from a stroke or heart attack. Though they didn't admit it, they didn't want to jeopardize their whole new program by having one of their first patients not survive the process, even if the procedure itself went without a mistake.

Their advice to me was to go home and get my affairs in order. At best, they said I had about five months to live.

Being only forty-one, what they told me really didn't sink in, at least, not at first. My wife and I knew we had hit a rough patch of sailing in our life, but, as of yet, we didn't really understand what was ahead. We had many plans for our future, and none of them had any time or room for this. After all, I had several real estate projects underway and had commitments to fulfill. I guess it started to soak in when we were driving home and we realized that we hadn't been asked to make any future appointments.

Still, at first, their verdict had less impact on me than I would have expected. Maybe it was because of the bone-numbing fatigue I was feeling after months of little or no sleep caused by my condition. I then began to wonder, even if I did beat this problem, will I be able to find real, lasting happiness in the years to come? I asked myself again and again, was life really just about having more new cars, airplanes, a bigger house and more vacations?

Chapter 3

Dying To Live

There is a time when death comes as softly as a dove in the night, whispering sweet things to those who wait.

Late Summer 1981

At the time I got the bad news from the medical team, I had never heard of sleep apnea as it was a newly diagnosed condition just appearing on the medical horizon. Of course it had always been around, but only then were specialists beginning to identify and recognize the part it played in the deaths of middle-aged men. My doctor had come to believe that most often when a man dies in his sleep, early in the morning, sleep apnea probably was the cause.

Even now, sleep apnea usually isn't recognized as a cause of death, as the death itself is oft times attributed to a stroke or heart attack. But, sleep apnea is usually the underlying cause.

in my case, the specialists told me that my apnea had been eroding my health for a long time, making me a prime candidate for an early death by stroke or heart attack. They were also beginning to surmise that sleep apnea was one of the reasons that women, on the average, live longer than men. For some inexplicable reason, sleep apnea is considerably more prevalent in men than women. It was their opinion that, over time, the longevity of men and women would equalize since the condition is now, easily treated.

I was suffering from an extreme case of *central nervous system sleep apnea* compounded by a second form, *obstructive sleep apnea*. The first form occurs in only 15% of sleep apnea cases and is akin to crib death in infants. For some unknown reason, at least unknown at that time, the body just forgets to breathe during deep REM sleep. The trachea, which we breathe through, is a hollow pipe consisting of a bundle of muscles held open by muscle tone. When some part of the autonomic nervous system "forgets" to maintain muscle tone in the trachea, the trachea collapses. Breathing through a collapsed trachea is a little like trying to sip a liquid through an old-fashioned paper straw that collapses when soaked with liquid. The part unknown, to the doctors at the time, was why the autonomic nervous system stopped sending signals to the trachea muscles, allowing it to collapse.

There is a second form of apnea, *obstructive apnea*, usually caused by obstructions in the throat, which block air passage during normal nighttime relaxation. This type of apnea is generally diagnosed with just a simple examination and confirmed by a sleep study. Now, thirty years later, Doctors routinely prescribe a C-Pap machine to assist breathing in both types of apnea.

However, the C-Pap machine hadn't been invented yet and I had both forms of apnea, and both were deadly. At the time there wasn't much doctors could do to relieve apnea, but they were experimenting with a somewhat radical form of surgery that they hoped would offer some relief. However, I hadn't qualified to be a participant in the operations, due to the deteriorated state of my health brought on by these advanced forms of apnea.

In today's world, patients with all types of sleep apnea respond well to C-Pap machines. This lifesaving apparatus saves thousands of lives each year by just putting positive air pressure into the trachea. Untreated sleep apnea, then or now, causes a deadly form of high blood pressure in the Pulmonary Circulatory System, which moves oxygenated blood from the lungs to the heart. This dangerous form of high blood pressure leads to heart attack or strokes. It is also the reason there are no telltale signs of the impending death of the victims. The only indication they might exhibit is that they may look dead tired. In fact, they may look as if they are "dying to get some sleep"...and they might well be.

During the first night I spent in the sleep lab, I stopped breathing over 200 times for durations of up to three and a half minutes at a time. You do the math. During a seven or eight-hour night, there wasn't much time when I was breathing or sleeping.

By this time, any joy in my life was long gone and matters only got worse over time. Sleeping in a bed was impossible. The only way I could get any sleep was upright in a chair. My life became a gray haze of hopelessness and suffering as I waited for the end. Eventually, I came to terms with my death for no other reason than the sleep it promised.

I was beginning to make peace with the fact that this world could go on without me. I knew my wife's petite, good-looks, betrayed a tough, resilient soul, who as a child, had already survived World War II and it's aftermath. With what we had accumulated, she and the girls would be alright after a while. Now, having put my affairs in order with an attorney, I was at peace, knowing that all was in order.

Since I held no spiritual beliefs, my Agnosticism provided the relief I needed. My belief that there was no God, therefore no heaven or hell, led me to believe that it would all be over when I died. Frankly, I looked forward to the oblivion *and the sleep* it would bring. I had no fear of death and what it would bring, since our reality is always shaped by our beliefs. Once I became comfortable with the idea of the world going on without me, I had nothing to fear. From the beginning, I had known my life was going to end this way eventually. It wasn't *if* I was going to die, it was just when. So, what difference would it make a thousand years from now?

Finally, I could sleep for a long, long time. It was incredible how appealing that thought became. While I hadn't reached the point of actually wanting to end it all myself, the idea of finally having plenty of sleep with eternal rest had a very strong appeal.

Chapter 4

Living To Die

*Sometimes a person can be lost
in the deluge of a "good life."*

Spring 1982

As I lost interest in living just as I had lost interest in the "good life," I am sure it felt like abandonment to my wife, and I understand why she would feel that way. Nonetheless, I was unsure what to do about it. She felt we should, in some way, be fighting harder against what was taking my life, but I didn't know how to do that. We were already in the hands of the best medical team possible, working on the cutting edge of this recently discovered new field of medicine. Stanford had already teamed up with its Japanese counterpart and they were in contact with similar efforts all over the world. Where were we supposed to go? Were we supposed to run off to some South American healer or witch doctor, whose stories never quite checked out? It seemed we were doing all we could do, and, at the time, I had complete faith in the American Medical Model and had no inner faith or guidance to fall back on.

The only consolation I had was that my wife and the girls would be in solid financial condition. Over the years, I had morphed from building student apartments to developing retail rental space, as well as, office buildings to lease to doctors and lawyers. They were all on long-term leases and easy to manage and our attorney would handle whatever my wife couldn't or didn't wish to deal with. Always a bright woman, she had actually become very knowledgeable in the business from managing our student apartments. At the time, I kept thinking she might be better off without me, and she could then get on with her life. In spite of it all, at some level, neither of us really understood the finality of what was happening in our lives or inside my body. I wasn't sick; I was just tired in a way that was hard to explain.

During that period, I spent most of my time falling asleep, then being rousing by my need for oxygen. During the day, there was almost an unreal quality to it all. I could be talking with my wife at the dinner table one moment and suddenly be asleep with my face in my plate the next. Driving was out of the question after I started wrecking cars faster than the insurance company could, or would, repair or replace them.

Being tired from the lack of sleep is uncomfortable. Being tired from lack of sleep over days or months is torturous. During the Korean War, both sides used sleep deprivation as a very effective way of breaking prisoners down and getting them to talk. Even today, in some places, it as one of the most powerful ways to get information from reluctant prisoners.

During my more lucid times, I seemed to derive pleasure from drifting back through old memories of earlier days when the future ahead of us was bright and life seemed alive with promise. Looking back on my life, all the years I had been so focused and sure of my goals, I really didn't begin to understand what was and wasn't actually relevant in life. In fact, now, facing death, most of what I had believed was important was proving to be trifling and insignificant. What difference did it really make if we had the newest and best of everything?

Sometimes on the edge of sleep, an odd kaleidoscope of old memories about seemingly unrelated experiences would swirl through my mind. It was as if I were being told, "Hey, you need to look at these; they are important." The same memories would play back as a reoccurring theme.

But why, after all, these years, would these particular experiences keep bubbling up, and how could they be important now? I had no idea. Because they were always there just as I drifted to sleep, I found myself using them as a distraction, as an escape from my suffering. Then I would often wonder how they could possibly be relevant to my eventual reality. Since I was rousing to breathe 200 times a night, it meant I drifted off to sleep often and spent a large part of my time in this reflective state.

The central theme that kept recurring were those of being under the thumb of my nemesis, my fifth-grade teacher. Sometimes this then merged with my being misplaced into a teaching role while in the army and discovering that education didn't have to be painful, after all. Then, there were reoccurring scenes from the few years I had spent developing a self-directed learning program for children who were bored or struggled in grade school as I did. Sometimes, in these moments of reflection, I wondered if those times weren't some of the most important elements of my life, instead of all the "things" I had accumulated. Was helping a small child turn their life around intrinsically of more value than owning a faster airplane that really didn't have any real purpose in my life anyway?

However, perhaps the most curious theme was my fascination with memories of being in Germany in the army, and being continually befriended or helped out by Germans who seemed vaguely familiar. In fact, some were so familiar that I tried past-life regression in an attempt to satisfy my curiosity. And, if I believed what we discovered, I had lived in Germany in a life time prior to this life.

My wife became curious, so she went with me to see what I was doing. Afterward she was quiet, which I misread as skepticism of what she had seen and heard. However, I was skeptical myself. Finally, she told me, "Duane, you spoke fluent German while you were under hypnosis, something you can't do when awake." That really baffled us. My speaking skills in German after being in Germany for four years remained elementary at best. It was just as the army had predicted with their entry assessment tests, as I rated in the bottom 3 percentile in the language………. assimilation part of the test.

In some ways, I guess we still kept expecting a miracle. But I did put my affairs in order. I also spent many hours in a semi-awake state, looking back over my life, trying to understand where I had gone wrong. How could I have all of these "things" after all my accomplishments and not care whether I lived or died? Was it a lack of sleep or something else. At this point, as I prepared to die, alive or dead, it didn't seem to make much difference any more. . It would all be over and relentless waves of time would wash away any trace of that brief moment in time when I had existed and built my sandcastles. I would be no more and I could finally sleep forever.

Chapter 5

The Four Horsemen Cometh

Tlot-tlot, tlot-tlot, in the distance!
Were they deaf that they did not hear?

—Alfred Noyes,
"The Highwayman"

June 1982

One early morning, in the darkest part of the night, just before the dawn, I sensed the end was near. Struggling to breathe for months had left me feeling that nothing else mattered anymore. With each day worse than the last, and tomorrow promising to be worse than today, all I wanted was relief at any cost. It had been this way ever since I had been given five months to live by a Stanford Medical Center doctor, and that was thirteen months ago.

For what seemed like a lifetime, I could either sleep or breathe, but not both at the same time. When I was

23

sleeping, I wasn't breathing, and when I was breathing, I wasn't sleeping. It had been several months since I had more than a few moments of sleep, snatched from between breaths. There is a reason why sleep deprivation was a favorite, age-old form of torture in some cultures and still is.

For some time now, the only way I could sleep at all was sitting upright in a chair, but even that was no longer working very well. In addition, the noise I made while trying to breathe made it impossible for my wife and I to be in the same room at night. Since my daughters also slept on the same floor and were light sleepers, I now slept in my office on a lower level. There, I would spend the night, sitting in my old recliner, propped straight up, trying to sleep. I was all alone early one morning when, between snatches of sleep and quick gasps for breath, I was suddenly falling through space. And I just kept falling, tumbling through a black sky, gripped with paralyzing, stark-naked terror. Instead of waking up, as I had in other "falling" dreams in the past, I just kept on falling and falling, tumbling out of control as I plummeted through the blackness.

Gradually, as I tumbled, I became aware of a soft light in one part of the black sky; my attention was drawn to the light, and it seemed to calm me. As I watched it, my attraction towards it grew stronger and stronger. Even though I was struggling to keep the light in my vision, the more I focused on it, the calmer I became. Then I realized I was falling toward the light.

The closer I came to the light, the brighter it grew. A warm feeling of peace and warmth began in my base chakra and spread upward through my entire body as the tumbling slowed.

On the distant horizon, silhouetted against the light, I saw what at first looked like an uneven line across the night-sky. As I drew closer, it grew into a line of people spanning the horizon. As they came out to greet me, backlit against the light, I knew them all. Some of them were from my life on earth, others were not.

There was my grandfather Amos, along with my favorite dog, Butch, his tail wagging in greeting, both central characters in the Rockwellian part of my childhood. There also was my wise old granddad Frank with his bemused wry grin. Included in this welcoming was my sweet ole' Aunt Eleanor and my favorite uncle, Sidney. There was even a man who lived on a ranch up river from us, who always had been kind to me, giving me a job, even when he really didn't need help. Finally, there was my favorite school teacher and various other people who had played a part in my life on earth but had gone on ahead.

As wonderful as it was to see those whom I lived with in my current life incarnation, there were others. There were also entities I had known and loved, from other times and other places, not from this incarnation.

As we all met, the warmth in the pit of my stomach continued to grow. Soon, I was flooded with the most intense feelings of love I had ever known, as it flowed through my core and back out to those around me. In a small way, it was like the "coming-home" feeling I had experienced back on earth as a younger man. I had been away from home for the first time, for three long years, in the army in Europe. As my rotation and discharge date neared, my feelings for being home, seeing my parents and eating mom's home cooked meals, grew to overshadow all else.

As I drove up the old familiar road to the ranch, that same teary-eyed "coming home" feeling began welling up in my throat, as I thought of mom and dad waiting there for me.. However, to compare that feeling with what I was now feeling, would be like comparing a drop of seawater to the entire ocean.

Chapter 6

A Triumphant Return

Home is the hunter home from the hill

—Robert Lewis Stevenson

June 1982

If I had thought death just led to oblivion, I was wrong. My death was not just falling asleep into a state of oblivion forever, but a waking up to a reality I couldn't imagine. As I was greeted by those I loved, I dissolved into the most intense love I had ever known. It rolled over me like the waves of a great tsunami, a happy, joyous love full of anticipation, promise, and closure. No words were exchanged, just thoughts moving instantaneously, with perfect clarity, from one eternal mind to another, without the ability to withhold or judge anything.

It was all an expression and celebration of love (which on earth was unfathomable), between members of an ancient soul group, celebrating the returning home of one of their own.

Slowly, as I looked at those gathered to greet me, I realized they were all there, not only from the life I had just left, but also from a prior life in Germany. I realized that the same souls have possibly played different parts in my many lives, sometimes being my daughter, my wife, or my mother. While at first this idea had startled me, but I soon realized, who was I to tell God what he could or couldn't do with his creations. Just because some Sunday school teacher had different ideas about how things worked, didn't really matter.

My joy deepened as I realized I had only left behind an earthly vestige of those I love, for the essence of each of those souls, was also here with me now. In addition to my friends and family of my most recent lifetime, there were the friendly Germans who had been hauntingly familiar while I was a young GI in Germany. Now I knew why they seemed so familiar at the time, they had been participants from a prior lifetime there.

I now understood that I had left nothing behind on earth. All my loved ones from that life, as well as all other incarnations, were here to greet me. All I had left behind were characters, playing a roles in a drama that we had choosen to play while our essence remained in the Afterlife. Now; it all seemed so simple.

As I was shown around, it was explained how most of our celestial, eternal knowledge is blanked out during our chosen life spans on earth. We must temporarily forget most of what our higher self already knows so we can immerse ourselves in the roles we have selected to play in our different lifetimes. Furthermore, I was told that it might take a while for all my knowledge and memories to return.

To ease my transition back into this realm, I was told to think of my time on earth as an extended visit to the ultimate theme park; consider it a place with thrilling rides and various adventures that we could choose to experience. I was also reminded the reason we leave the celestial realm at all, was for the excitement, variety, adventure, and entertainment that different incarnations offer.

However, to take all our Inner, Celestial, God-given knowledge with us on our various adventures, would have ruined the very experience we had chosen. I was advised to think of our trips to other realms as if choosing a new novel to read. We pick a new book depending on what we are in the mood to read. Furthermore, if we knew every twist and turn of the story, line-by-line prior to reading it, it would spoil the fun.

As one entity jokingly remarked, if the eternal and divine part of us grows tired of singing and playing harps, there are thousands of other universes available for our spiritual growth, amusement, and entertainment. As it says in The Course in Miracles, "We are only here for three reasons; to remember who we are; to help others remember who they are and . . . to enjoy the trip, . . . unless, of course, (we) use

29

our free will and chose not to." And, then he said again, "eternity is a long time to do nothing but play harps."

As my orientation went on, it was explained how, on this celestial side of the veil, anything we desire is instantaneously provided. We just need to feel a desire to have something, and it is fulfilled. But, therein lies the reason for all the realms outside of heaven. Having everything we want always develops, within us, a desire for variety and change for a challenge. It would be like a game in which everyone was a winner. Soon, the game would become boring, and we would look for another, more challenging one.

Somehow, all this sounded familiar. To demonstrate the process of instantaneous fulfillment, one of them asked me to think about something I really desired. Thinking back on it, what I chose seemed odd for such an esteemed place, and such a monumental event. But suddenly, I had an urge for a piece of my mother's famous homemade dark chocolate cake, with her unique fudge frosting. As soon as I thought of it, my earthly mother was handing me the biggest piece of dark chocolate cake I had ever seen. Dare I say it was heavenly?

Although she appeared there with us, I knew some part of her was still back on earth because she was not one who had gone on before. My guess was that she, at that very moment, was probably asleep, dreaming of lovingly making her son a piece of her divine chocolate cake.

After what could have been a few minutes or hours of orientation, a deep silence began to descend over everything. An all-encompassing "Presence" overshadowed the soul group as its members faded into the background. It was like being in a supermarket where music is playing in the background as you shop. Suddenly the volume fades and a voice, overshadowing the music, says, *"Welcome back Shoppers, on aisle #7 there is a great special on Red Delicious apples."* However, in this case, as everything else around me faded, a voice, which really wasn't a voice at all, said in resonating tones, "Welcome home son, you've done a great job."

Again, I was bathed in yet an even deeper, more profound sense of love and acceptance, that just kept growing stronger as the voice went on to say: "But as long as you still have a warm body back on earth, would you like to get another lifetime out of the way? You have some important commitments coming up in an earthly drama you, and one of your daughters, wrote."

I knew what was being asked instantly, even though at the time of my death I hadn't believed in any form of reincarnation or anything religious or spiritual. In spite of that, I instantly knew I was being asked if I wanted to return to the earth drama I had just left.

Now my Sunday school teacher had always told us that there is no pain in heaven. I can tell you now, at least, in that case, she was wrong. I can still hear the agony of my echoing "Nooooo" still rattling around somewhere in those celestial realms.

I knew in my heart of hearts, in the deepest core of my soul, that after escaping *"the surly bonds of earth to touch the face of God,"* as the poet John Gillespie Magee put it, I wanted no part of going back. After experiencing what I was experiencing in heaven, in no way did I want to go back to *that place* anytime soon. If it was a theme-park, they could keep any part of my "unused ticket" that was leftover. I had had enough drama for one lifetime. I was finished with that petty, trite, hellhole of a world, and all it represented to me at the time.

Naturally, my view of reality had slipped in the last part of my current adventure. It was as if I had gotten my foot stuck in the track of the roller coaster, the cars were coming and I didn't know how to free it.

Even if there were people back in my life on earth, who in earthly terms I loved as dearly as conditions there allowed, I wanted no part of that life now. From my current vantage point, I could see how trivial that world had been. Here, on the other side, I would always be with souls who had loved me from the beginning of time and will continue to do so forever. Plus, I now knew that the loved ones who lagged behind on earth would join us momentarily. It might be years waiting for them, but it would only be moments in reality. Time is funny that way from a celestial point of view.

"The Voice," with a tone of infinite patience and wisdom, went on to say, "One of the reasons you went to that planet to begin with, was your commitment to bringing your daughters, Christy and Traci, on board. Both are old souls, they have some important work to do as part of my unfolding plan. Would you leave them fatherless at their young age?"

What can a father say? Even if I thought I was already detaching from that life, apparently, there were deeper cords and promises of which I wasn't conscientiously aware. I instantly knew I would be returning, whether it was what I wanted at this moment or not. Then, as I was, metaphorically "going out the door," The Voice continued. "Since you are going to be there for a while, there are a couple of things you could do for me, as you grow inward. But, don't worry; I'll have your Soul Guides send you a great little guidebook to get you started on your next adventure in that life."

Chapter 7

The Early Years

There is no place so magical
as this world to a small child

1940 to 1946

Born on a farm along the banks of Williams Creek in the Applegate Valley in Southern Oregon, I lived the first six years of my life in a small white house nestled under several spreading oak trees. This place I called home was located on a small farm halfway between two general stores in the wee hamlet of Williams, Oregon.

Across the main road from our house was a small sawmill. It was here at the mill, where dad and granddad, along with ten or twelve other men cut lumber during World War II for the war effort. In those days, if you operated a small sawmill, you usually also owned the timber, did the logging, and hauled the logs to the mill. After cutting the logs into lumber, you sold it in the lumberyard by the sawmill or hauled it to the railhead for shipment to some army depot.

Until I was six, the farm and lumber mill were my playground and universe, as I was surprisingly free to roam them at will. Some of my fondest memories come from this time of my life. My bedroom was accessed through a narrow stairway in the attic just above the kitchen. In the morning, I would awake to the aroma of mouth-watering bacon, eggs, and pancakes drifting up the narrow stairs. Then the sounds of my granddad's booming laughter would filter through the house and upstairs as he and my father came in from the morning chores at the barn.

Each morning, before breakfast, they milked and fed the animals and harnessed the teams of horses to be used later in the day at the mill. As I heard them entered the kitchen, I would get up, wiping sleep from my eyes as I tottered down the stairs. There, granddad would scoop me up, hoisting me to the ceiling, setting me on is shoulders where he would fly me around the room. "Grandad," actually wasn't my real granddad, he was my dad's uncle Amos, who had raised dad after his mother died when dad was three. "So, Amos was my favorite, and only "granddad" and was a natural part of my young life. Little did I know what that would mean, later.

Amos, who was my best pal at that age, was a giant-hearted man whose laughter was infectious. He was always dressed in clean bib overalls, except when he went to church, which wasn't often. He was a natural magnet for kids, dogs and other animals, a regular *Pied Piper* to them all. He was a larger-than-life person in a small community and I adored him. He also seemed to have a strong affection for me. Maybe it was because he had no children of his own, but mostly, it was because, as I would later understand, he was one of my Soul Guides.

Amos was a giant in my world and helped shape the person I became, as well as the values I later embraced. He was someone who paid little attention to money, and seemed to have a natural ability to make it by the wheelbarrow loads, and then give it away as fast as he made it.

As a child, I was lucky also to have another loving "grandfather" in my early life. However, he didn't appear until my grandmother died, and he then moved to the ranch from California. In retrospect, Frank, my mother's father, was one of the oldest souls I ever met. If he wasn't a real, honest-to-goodness saint, he didn't miss by much. With his bemused, enigmatic smile always playing across his face, it seemed impossible for him to see or believe anything bad in any person or situation. It was only much later in my life that I came to realize what he already knew long before I was born. It would take me forty years and a Near Death Experience to even begin to grasp what he knew then.

Later, I realized these two men were part of an almost magical force in my life. They were just first of a number of elderly men who were always around at the right place and the right time. During my younger years, I had no way of understanding how lucky I was to have two such grandfathers as I grew up.

My memories of those early mornings are cast in a magical time of innocence and childhood dreams. On those magical mornings, I ate in my pajamas, alongside my dad and granddad. Mom was always busy, plying us with course after course, all but a few basics, grown and prepared by hands that loved me. Mother viewed the world; her job was to see that her family wouldn't face a long day on an empty stomach. There was always plenty of fresh-squeezed juice, real oatmeal, pancakes, ham or steak, eggs, biscuits, and toast, always topped off our breakfast with something baked. It might be a cinnamon roll or coffee cake, with plenty of milk to go with it, fresh from the barn, with a cream line partway down the pitcher. That was the way breakfast was in those days in our house, in the days before machinery replaced muscle power, and men consumed piles of food when it was available.

Chapter 8

The Lumber Mill

For a small boy born free,
the entire world is his classroom

1944-46

In those years, after breakfast, my dad and granddad would follow the path across the field and climb the wooden steps of the stile, straddling the fence along the highway. On the other side, the path led to a log pond where it became a series of floating logs, chained end to end, with a walking surface hewn flat on their top-side. Once they crossed the log pond and entered the mill, they began the second part of their workday.

Back at the house, as soon as dad and Amos left, I would gobble the rest of my breakfast, run upstairs and hurriedly dress. Then, I would plead with my mother to be allowed to follow after my heroes. On lucky days, and that was most days as I grew a little older, I was off down the path, over the stile, and across the road to the log pond. Here, I would pick up my own pike-pole, just like the longer ones used by the men to move the floating logs, but one cut shorter for me. Then, I would continue on across the log bridge to the sawmill. There, I would usually go underneath it where my Uncle Harry already had a roaring fire in the boiler that drove the steam engine. He was "building-a-head-of-steam," as it was called in the days of steam-driven machinery. At 8:00 o'clock Uncle Harry would blow the ear-piercing, steam whistle, signaling the beginning of a long day of sawing logs into lumber. The steam engine was the heart of the mill, driving the huge saw and moving the log carriage back and forth across the saw blade.

Being at the tail end of the steam era, if something moved or turned, it still took a horse, a man, or a steam engine. If a log needed rolling over, or a piece of lumber needed moving, muscle power of either a man, a horse or a steam engine did the job.

The steam engine, which seemed as large as a locomotive to a five-year-old boy, was about the only source of mechanical power around the mill. Since the steam boiler burned wood scraps from the mill and electricity was still new in rural America, the mill wasn't even wired for electric.

In the last year of the war, as more lumber was needed by the Army, Uncle Harry wired a few bare light bulbs in the mill. Now they could saw before full daylight, and as light faded at night, cutting lumber a few more hours each day.

With that, they felt they were doing their part to help the men overseas.

The underbelly of the mill fascinated me. I wanted to know what made it all work. After a while of watching and asking Uncle Harry endless questions, I would go on to other parts of the mill, driven by a young boy's insatiable curiosity.

For the rest of the day, I usually had free run of most of the mill and mill yard, though one part of the mill yard was absolutely off-limits to me. It was a pile of burning sawdust the size of a large house, left over from the saws. And, having been provided with ample stories of young children who perished in craters of burning sawdust, I took heed.

Later, as an adult, I questioned whether I would have allowed a son of mine such freedom at such a young age. I questioned for a while whether my parents had been negligent or not. It was only later that I realized my parents weren't negligent; I had probably just fallen in the crack between Mom's world and Dad's, at least at first.

Mom probably sent me off to the mill to go be with my dad, assuming he would keep an eye on me, which he always did. Then, when he sent me back to the house, sometimes, I would stop and see Amos along the way. As time went by, Mom probably thought I was with Dad, and Dad often would think, I was with Mom. This way I often slipped through a crack and was off somewhere else. After a while, they seemed to decide that since I survived, I must be safe. Soon, I was free to roam all day long.

Now, as I look back, it is easy to believe something or someone was watching over me. I was relatively free, at a young age, in what was a potentially dangerous environment. However, I believe my later self-reliance came from learning to extract myself from the little scrapes and jams a boy of that age manages to get into. Furthermore it's possible that learning many of life's lessons early, in age-appropriate doses, allows one to avoid many larger pitfalls, later-on. Or, as I now believe, my soul guides were very busy at the time.

Chapter 9

A Rockwellian Childhood Goes Awry

Into each life, a little rain must fall

—Henry Wadsworth Longfellow

1950 - 1960

I had entered school on top of the world, eager to learn everything there was to know, in an era before teachers knew about dyslexia. My natural confidence and verbal abilities carried me well through the fourth grade. Before my fifth year of school, my teachers seemed to accept me and my odd style of writing. I had developed a method of printing because cursive writing, for me, was impossible. My fingers just wouldn't cooperate. I did my homework as required, and usually received an A or B in most subjects. Nevertheless, in the fifth grade, my charmed world came crashing down around me. At that time, I met a teacher

43

who was a real life changer—in a negative way, or so it seemed at the time.

I remember her as a self-righteous, frustrated woman who thought the way to motivate children, little boys in particular, was to shame them into better performance. Her favorite form of motivation used on children struggling to write legibly was to hold the offending work up for the class to ridicule. Then, she would post it on a special bulletin board for all to examine as an example of what she didn't want. If her efforts created any reaction from the child, she only increased the pressure.

Her favorite punishment was "detention sentences" for work not meeting her "standards," and mine never did, try as I might. As a punishment, she would write a sentence consisting of thirty to thirty-five words in length on the blackboard, tailored to admonish me for the error of my ways and sloppy penmanship. (Penmanship loomed large in her mind, and no messy printing was allowed!)

For the first offense, she would have me copy, in longhand, a hundred of these sentences during my recesses or lunchtime. For a young boy of ten, who struggled to shape each letter individually one at a time, the punishment of a hundred such sentences was akin to capital-punishment. In addition, any sentences not completed the first day carried over to the recesses of the next. Sometimes, she would reject the whole assignment if she thought my penmanship looked like I "wasn't trying hard enough."

By the time I completed the first 100 sentences, I usually had earned another 200 or 300 sentences. The magical life I had experienced until then, began to turn gray and dark. The worst of it was that it all seemed to be my fault. I thought maybe I wasn't trying hard enough or maybe I was lazy.

To add insult to injury, my older sister had been in her class a few years earlier, usually receiving straight A's. Because of this, I consistently heard, "Why can't you be like your sister? You're capable; you just aren't trying hard enough; you don't care." As time went on, she acted as if I was underperforming just to spite her. In time, I became angry and sullen, believing there was nothing I could do to please her.

To make matters even worse, often I would grasp a difficult problem that others were struggling with, in science or math, and figure it out my own way. But, instead of being praised for my work, the teacher would accuse me of cheating. Alternately, if I hadn't done it the way the teacher thought it was supposed to be done, that too made me wrong, and in time, I began to give up.

When reports from my teacher came home saying, "Duane is not applying himself." Or alternately, "Duane copying the work of others," I began to question myself and think maybe it was my fault; maybe I wasn't working hard enough. While I knew I wasn't copying anything, I began to question why I couldn't do things "right." I started to wonder what was wrong with me.

45

For awhile, I would start each day determined to try harder and work harder. But, try as I might, I just couldn't make the letters on the paper come out right, or in their proper order. In addition, I often couldn't come to the right math answer in the same way other kids did. Of course, this caused me further grief when I couldn't always articulate the often circuitous way that I arrived at my answers. To top it all off, hours of struggling created a messy paper, ripped from all the erasures. Often, when finished, I couldn't read my own writing, no matter how hard I tried to be neat, or how determined I was to do better. Slowly, I began to give up in despair.

Whatever the cause, as I gave in to the shame and anger, it all turned into resistance and then rebellion. As time went on, I no longer even bothered to do classroom work unless the teacher stood over me and forced me. Homework was out of the question. It was easier to take the pain of, not doing something than the shame and ridicule of doing it poorly or being accused of cheating.

Looking back at it now from a metaphysical viewpoint, what was happening to me at the time was necessary and perfect, preparing me for a role I was preparing for later on. But, of course, I couldn't see it at the time.

Later, an ability to understand failing kids and to feel their pain, helped me realize it isn't always just the kids fault. In addition, I realized that it is almost never a lack of native intelligence. After all, they had mastered their native language, the most difficult thing a human ever masters prior to entering school, without the help of a teacher or lesson plans. As an adult who has struggled with his own language and a couple of foreign ones as well, it makes all five-year-olds sound like geniuses, to me.

40 years later, I would realize that my hated fifth-grade teacher prepared me well for one of the roles I had chosen for this incarnation, one which would, play a direct part in my NDE (NDE Experience). Yet it is still difficult to say, *Thank you,* Mrs. G...

While writing, grammar, and spelling were nearly impossible to me, reading, itself, was easy. Because of my good verbal skills and reading ability, I was continually passed on to higher grades. In high school, the results of my written work were much the same. Classes that required writing continued to be extremely frustrating. Math, science, and physics were easy for me; however, with my odd way of figuring things out, I still often had trouble seeing how others arrived at the same answers that I did. However, I would usually receive an A or B for my work in those classes if the teachers weren't big on homework. But, my attitude problem carried over, and I refused to do anything outside of the classroom. If I couldn't do it during class time, I didn't do it.

Somehow, I was able to graduate on time, although in the bottom third of my class. In addition, since I came from a family of Scotch and Irish forefathers who were either hellfire and brimstone preachers or schoolteachers, there was no doubt that I would go to college. That concept was so thoroughly ingrained in my upbringing that I really didn't even question the idea.

However, after a short stint in college, my inability to write and my poor study habits, along with my partying, finally caught up with me. I had become a regular visitor to the Dean's office and he eventually asked me to leave. When my father found out of my dismissal, he negotiated my reinstatement. However, the next time I was called into the Dean's office, he assured me that a visit from my father wouldn't help this time. Furthermore, he said that, were I to ever apply to reenter school, even if I waited fifty years, I would still be on social probation.

By now, my father also realized the futility of what he was trying to do, and quietly said, "Son, I think you better go into the army and grow up." When he said that, I'm sure he didn't know what a relief that it was to me, and once again, the timing was perfect. Had I left school a week later, everything would have unfolded differently, and I would have missed two pivotal events that changed my life forever.

A series of events from the fifth grade onward set a pattern that repeated over and over in my life. Something or someone always saw to it that I was where I needed to be, just when I needed to be there, ready for the next lesson in life.

My father's suggestion had been wise counsel. At the time, I had been thinking about my options, and the army appealed to my sense of adventure, but I didn't know how to approach my dad on the subject. So when he suggested it, I agreed to "join the army and see the world," which was the recruiting slogan at that time.

However, I left college for the army, feeling like I had a big "D" for "dumb" branded across my forehead, feeling like maybe I was the dumbest person in the world. I guess I knew that I wasn't actually "dumb", but I had no idea what was wrong with me. My self-esteem was about as low as it could be. However, in retrospect, I can now see that I, luckily, hadn't lost my fighting spirit. That, as I found out later as a teacher, is truly when a child is in trouble.

Chapter 10

A Life-Changing Coincidence

*Sometimes we even think we are
in control of our destiny.*

1960

As with many young men who struggled in school, military duty has proven to be what I needed. It was in the army where my self-esteem began returning. It was there I began to question some of my false assumptions about myself and schools I had acquired along the way.

Probably the first morale booster was the induction process, and the testing done by the army before my training began. At the time of my enlistment, half the draftees called up, failed the army's entry-level testing and, for this reason, weren't eligible for military duty. That meant that half the men in America, including high school graduates and dropouts and those who avoided school altogether, were flunking the high school equivalency test.

After three days of rigorous testing, to my surprise, I scored well overall. In fact, in a few areas, I ranked in the 97 percentile of all who had passed the test.

This seemed strange to me, as I had a misconception that how "smart" I was or wasn't, in some way related to my schooling. Since I had, at least mentally, dropped out in the fifth grade, and hadn't participated in school much after that, I assumed, if tested, I would test at a fourth-grade level.

Now I was puzzled. I had aced the Army's high school equivalency test when half of the men being drafted didn't. It was the first crack to appear in my view of school and my abilities to survive it. It was a morale booster, the first "wind beneath my wings" of my battered deflated ego, in a long time.

However, in one area of the test related to Language Assimilation, I failed miserably, ranking in the lowest 3% of those taking the test. Later, I realized that probably this was what had tripped me up in school, making writing and grammar so difficult.

Lucky for me, my reading, and oral skills were intact. These skills left me reading at a college level in grade school. In addition, I was well coordinated physically in all areas, but, for some reason, my brain just could not get my fingers to form written letters. I was devoid of an ability to spell, understand grammar, or punctuate a sentence. Maybe this explains why, as a kid, it was more important to be able to throw a slider in a ball game than spell the word "slider" for a spelling test.

The largest boost to my morale, however, was caused by something else the army does well—get things mixed up. For some unfathomable reason, I was assigned to an Army experimental program being conducted by the University of Maryland for the army. However, it was not only that I was posted to the University of Maryland, *but as a teacher*. It would be years before I realized that this stroke of fate was, again, intervention by a higher power, making sure I was in the right place at the right time. I was being provided with just what I needed for the role I had chosen to play during this extended incarnation.

The army had drafted 350 men who had, somehow, avoided any schooling. These weren't dropouts, these were adults who had never darkened the door of a classroom. Because of that fact, the Army assumed they were illiterate.

Apparently, the College of Education of the University, after studying self-educated people of history, was now seeking better ways to educate children. They knew that many of the great people in history, many who had changed the world, had little or no formal schooling.

Apparently, they didn't consider George Washington or Benjamin Franklin illiterate just because they had little formal education beyond early grade school. Nor did they feel Henry Ford, the Wright Brothers, Thomas Edison, Walt Disney, or Albert Einstein illiterate or uneducated.

However, how and where did they become educated? And was it applicable to a modern world?

Aware of the number of men who were ineligible for military duty because of a lack of literacy, the University approached the army, wanting them to fund an experiment with these men. They wanted to see if it were possible to bring them to a point of literacy.

The army, was trying to determine if these men could be "educated" to a high school equivalency so they could be eligible for military service, and, if so, how long it would take.

By the time I became part of the process, they had already attempted a similar program on groups of high school dropouts. That attempt had failed miserably. However, designers of the experiment, now, thought they knew why.

The dropouts who were given a new "opportunity" to finish school already "knew" they hated school and weren't interested in more of the same thing. It seemed they had developed an attitude toward school similar to mine.

At this point, the program had been modified for men who had never been to school at all. This was the point where lightning had struck, and I was assigned by the Army to the University of Maryland *as a teacher in their experimental program.*

Of course, the army is notorious for their mix-ups and it is due to these mix-ups that the origination of the familiar acronym SNAFU, short for *Situation Normal, All F....d Up,* originated. However, it was due to an Army SNAFU, that put me right where the Infinite Intelligence had been sending me, all along.

When I reported for duty, I knocked on the door of the OIC, Officer in Charge. Responding to a gruff, "Come in," I found myself standing in front of a Major. Without looking up from his paperwork, he said, "Yes, soldier?"

I said, "Sir, there's been a mistake. It says on my set of orders, I am assigned as a teacher to your company. Sir, I'm not qualified to be a teacher, not by a long shot."

Without stopping what he was doing, he said, "Soldier, do you enjoy KP and guard duty?"

I said, "No, sir."

His reply surprised me when he said, "Good, you qualify."

I tried to tell him of my troubles in school, and while he softened a little, he just said, "Don't worry about it, soldier; the University knows what it's doing."

"B-but, sir—" I stammered, but he cut me off.

"Look soldier, the army was supposed to send me qualified teachers, but the army doesn't always get it right, and it's too late to correct it now because classes start Monday. However, I looked at your test scores, and you'll do fine. The instructor doesn't have to know the subject. The material is put together to do the teaching. Your job is just to sit in the classroom, hand out the material, and keep an eye on the clock, for breaks. Can you do that?"

"Yes sir," I replied, knowing it was time to leave but not entirely sure of the situation I was getting into. Nevertheless, I decided to go along with the ruse. After all, getting off KP and guard duty was worth the risk.

The first surprise was how average these supposedly illiterate men were. In general conversation and by all appearances, they were just like everyone else I knew. Plus, they were interested in learning. They saw this as an opportunity they hadn't had for various reasons.

The next thing that surprised me was how simple and logical the material was, as well as the way it was presented. They called the method *Programmed Learning*, and the men took to it immediately. They worked their way through the material at their own individual pace with plenty of breaks and no pressure in a relaxed and congenial atmosphere.

There was little need for me to do anything, except hand out the day's work and occasionally show a movie called for in my instructions. Otherwise, all I had to do was stand there looking "teacherly." The key was the material and how it was presented. The fact that I wasn't qualified to teach math didn't matter because the subject matter wasn't dependent on me as a teacher. The material and its arrangement was the key. It was simple and direct, and the men loved it.

I always felt that part of the reason for its success was because these men had something I had lost by the fifth grade—a belief that learning could be fun and exciting. These men didn't even want to quit at break time! But then they hadn't been through the same dull, boring book-driven lessons, day after, boring, day for twelve long, tiresome years. Of course, this is also why this program had so little success when, first used on high school dropouts.

Dropouts had resisted it from the onset. In their belief, it was just more of the same old BS, so naturally, they wouldn't give it a chance. As we know, there are "none so deaf as those who will not hear, none so blind as those who will not see."

I worked with these men an hour a day, and the rest of the day, they took other high school equivalency classes. As the days turned into weeks, probably what impressed me the most, was the sheer excitement and enthusiasm they had for the material even though it was rather basic.

The results didn't surprise me. By the time we reached the end of the ninety days allotted for the class, 92% of them had passed their GED test. These men conquered the equivalent of twelve years of math while, at the same time, learned a full range of other subject materials as well. They earned a high school GED diploma, covering grade 1 through grade 12, in just ninety days. This, to me, was extraordinary. And, that was the way they felt too like they had conquered something. I don't believe I have ever met a prouder bunch of GIs. They had just slain a personal dragon in ninety days.

After being part of that program and seeing how well it worked, I was left feeling cheated and conned. If these men could get the equivalent of a twelve-year education in ninety days, it made me question the twelve years I had spent in dull, boring classrooms. When I thought of what I learned in my twelve years, compared with these men, I didn't seem to have anything they didn't have, except a bad attitude and hatred for schools.

Those ninety days were pivotal to me in what was to come after my army experience. This learning and teaching experience did a lot to restore my belief in myself and to shape my future attitudes toward education. For now, I knew there was a better way. And, of course, later, I would discover that it was part of the very reason I came to this planet.

However, before leaving the Army and Germany, I repeatedly met people and experienced events, which didn't fit with what I had learned in the short time I was in Sunday school, as a child.

Chapter 11

Déjà Vu or Something Else

We never know when real magic is afoot

1960-64

While I was in the army in Germany in the sixties, about fifteen years after WWII, I experienced incidents that I couldn't begin to understand from the Baptist perspective with which I was raised. Once the cracks in my old belief structure began to widen, I began having more questions, than answers. Soon, I saw a world that was very different the one described by my Sunday school teacher.

After I had left church as a teenager, I hadn't given much thought to spiritual matters, at least not beyond the lesson of Sunday School that had been spoon-fed, then rejected. In Germany, I kept having soul-shaking incidents of déjà vu that left me seeking answers to questions of which I'd never had to consider. Furthermore, I soon realized that I would never find answers to these questions in the old

Southern Baptist brand of born-again religion I had been exposed to as a child.

Why, on my second day in Germany, at six o'clock in the morning, would a twenty-year-old GI in full military gear, suddenly be stricken with blinding terror? Why, would I suddenly be struggling to get free of my captors, who were only the other GIs I was traveling with?

Just moments before, we had been GIs on a train coming from the northern German port of Bremerhaven, south into central Germany where we were to be stationed. Then, as we entered the train station in the city of Frankfurt, and we started to disembark, a wave a panic swept over me like a stiff wind over dry leaves. . *Suddenly, I knew I had been here before, and suddenly it was then and not now.* In an instant, all the uniforms around me were the enemy I was struggling desperately to escape from. Frantically, as I shoved and kicked, a voice cut through the terror, one I recognized as a friend, then the reality of 1960 postwar Germany came back into focus.

As I struggled to regain my composure, I couldn't help but notice the stares of my buddies around me, as they tried to figure out what had just happened. Fortunately for me, in the rush of getting off the train, the incident was forgotten, as most of us went our own ways. Why, a few weeks later, would I, without a thought, dive for cover at the sight of the first German army tank I encountered in the German countryside while on NATO Maneuvers?

Why did I keep meeting German citizens ten or fifteen years my elder who seemed beyond just familiar? Sometimes, we would talk and sometimes not. We would both be curiously drawn to each other. Often, we could barely understand each other's language, but we knew there was a strong draw for some reason I couldn't fathom.

In addition, why did strangers often seem to appear out of nowhere, offering help just when I needed it most? Sometimes, it was a motorist on the Autobahn when my car was broken down, or just someone who would point out the trail on a mountain trek? Why did a series of seemingly random, although synchronistic events keep happening to me, that now, even forty years later, still define my life? Little did I realize the answers were somewhere in another lifetime, that would take twenty more years of living and death, to sort out.

At the time, I didn't think much about these incidents. I just relegated them to some little-used part of my mind where I stored things that really didn't make sense. It was only later, as these incidents began to stack up, that I felt compelled to consider them.

Years and a death later, as I gained a broader view of reality, I realized that many of these people were people I had known in my prior life, in Germany, who were still alive in my current incarnation, and whose lives overlapped this current one. However, at the time, I was far from understanding or believing such things. That was something that would required a new perspective.

Since then, I have wondered what my years in Germany would have been like had I realized that my feelings of déjà vu were indicative of my living in Germany, before. But, I had no answers because I didn't even know the question.

Much later, it became apparent that those experiences were, again, preparation for what lie ahead. It was an introduction to something I would have thought to be nonsense at the time. Yet, it planted a seed. In many ways, those three years were essential to whom I would become, the basis of what was to happen to me, and why I was on this planet.

Chapter 12

Drawn to Europe

*We never know when our life
is about to change forever.*

1962

The most life-changing of all the serendipitous events that happened to me occurred after my scheduled tour in Europe was over. Just before my departure date, the Berlin Crisis flared up, and we all had our duty tours extended for an extra six months. During this period, on one Friday night, another sergeant and I were out on the town to drown our sorrows about having our tours of duty extended. Late that evening, as I was driving back to the base, my friend wanted to stop for a late-night pizza and one last beer. I tried to dissuade him, as I didn't need another beer and wasn't hungry at the time. I just wanted to go to bed. My friend wasn't to be denied, so I finally agreed. Little did I realize that it was one of those small decisions that would alter my life forever. While we were eating our pizza, I noticed a pair of beautiful dark eyes from far across the room. Those eyes haunted me, regardless of the fact she was with a couple of friends, unaware I was in the room. At that moment, the girl waiting for me back home, lost all her charm to a girl I hadn't even met, yet.

I asked around and found out she was a German girl and that her parents forbade her even to talk to GIs. Because of that, it took nearly two months just to meet her, let alone get a date with her. However, from that first night, I felt something I had never felt before; Fate had once again rolled the dice.

Again, something larger than myself was at play. Had it not been for a whole series of events lining up that day in just the right order at just the right time, everything in my life would have unfolded differently. Likewise, without some of the events that it led up to it, my Near Death Experience would have just been my death. If so, I would have never returned to my current life, this book would never have been written, and you would now be doing something else with your time.

At the time, I had no way of knowing that a late-night, spur-of-the-moment decision to stop for pizza would change my life forever. Now, more than fifty years later, the ripple effects of that quick decision are still altering my life. Since you are reading this book, that decision made so long ago will now change *your* future in some small way, whether or not you believe it is. Let me explain.

After reading for a while, you may decide to stop and go to the store. At this point, when you choose to stop reading seems your choice and an arbitrary one at that. Then, depending on that whim, you might or might not meet an old friend on the way. You might talk with them for a few minutes, or longer. Either way, the rest of your day will unfold differently, than if you had stopped reading five minutes later or earlier, and missed your friend altogether.

In addition, when we "accidently" bump into different people, we also change the seemingly random patterns of their day also, and eventually they affect others they meet. Someone may avoid an accident they might otherwise have been involved in, or someone may have an accident they wouldn't have had if they had been a minute earlier or later. And the ripple effects continue, outward, forever. While I had always disregarded this logic as trivial, it became apparent to me, that my little unimportant decisions allow me to make an important one. . . or not.

But, serendipity happens not only at the moment I happen to stop reading a book; but from the ten thousand other little snap decisions I make every day without thinking or noticing. It's been said in many ways, by many sages, that *life is the sum of your little choices that make possible the large choices.*

I always believed that I put a great deal of careful thought into making major life decisions. However, I soon realized that the actual essence of my life had been built on a thousand small choices I had made, conscious or unconscious, interwoven with synchronistic events that were beyond my control. Looking back, I realize that even without much Inner Guidance at the time, all seemed to have worked out pretty well. Once I had grasped this idea, I wondered what my life would be like, had all my choices, small and large, been made from a place of Inner Guidance instead of my being led around by an ego-driven, monkey mind.

At the time I was in the Army in Germany, I believed that I and I alone controlled my choices. I no longer believe that. I have come to realize that thousands of minor synchronistic coincidences every minute of our lives shape our larger decisions. I have come to understand that we all are far more powerful than we realize. Every little decision keeps on affecting us and those around us positively or negatively for years. I have an old new-age friend who is right when he says, "*What goes around, comes around and pats us on the back or bites us in the butt.*"

All humanity's most vaulted endeavors are destined for the dust heaps of history. In a few thousand years, even Boulder Dam will be little more than a pile of washed sand and gravel. In ten thousand years, the Pyramids of Egypt will follow. There is only one thing that people do that lasts forever—make a choice, the ripple effects of which last forever.

Is it possible that God created us in his image as infinitely powerful beings who, without knowing, change the world with each thought or action, whether it be a positive or negative thought? Could it be that the condition of our own world is a result of our choices, whether coming from ego or Divine Guidance?

Chapter 13

Marriage, a Life Changer

"To really live you must almost die."

—Gary Cooper, from the movie,
The Hanging Tree

June 1963 – 1980

A few months after finally receiving my discharge from the army, I had gone back to Germany to marry the girl from the serendipitous meeting in the pizza parlor. Now, in hindsight of an afterlife perspective, I realize she was one of the reasons I had gone to Germany in the first place—to meet her and some of our friends from another life.

After a time in Germany, we returned stateside, settling in the small college town of Ashland, Oregon. There, I worked at various jobs and, eventually, with great trepidation, began taking some entry-level college courses. At first, I migrated to the Psychology Department, probably in an attempt to understand what was wrong with me that had made grade school so difficult. I eventually ended up in the Education Department. Here, classes in early childhood development and alternate methods of learning started to shed some light on my learning difficulties.

While in college, I began a small construction company and began converting old houses into student apartments. By the time I graduated, I had accumulated a number of college rentals and excellent monthly income, and I continued to add extra apartments as I could afford to do so. Nevertheless, for a while, the itch to be a teacher for was growing. I just wanted to teach long enough to test some of my theories, and, with my apartments, I had some flexibility.

So, with a diploma in hand, I started looking for a teaching job. Of course, once again, I had no idea that Providence was shuffling my daily itinerary to put me exactly where the higher part of me wished to be. Of course, all the while, I thought I was operating strictly on my mortal mind's free will.

Soon, I was a first-year teacher with a room full of fifth graders. I immediately began implementing a rather unproven and unorthodox bag of tricks. Out went the desks; in came worktables, a few old sofas, and rugs, as well as an ancient but working refrigerator and hot plate. By Christmas, the principal had had enough of my methods and made no bones about it.

One afternoon, the principal, along with the superintendent, paid my room an unexpected visit. As they left, the Superintendent asked me to come to his office after class. With that, I knew my days as a teacher at that school were now over.

After school, I packed up the few personal things I would take with me, some mementos of the kids, and a few pictures and put it all in my car.

I entered the superintendent's lair like a condemned man; his secretary eyed me warily as she spoke into the intercom. Then she gestured down the hall, and I took that to mean I was to walk the last mile alone.

The superintendent met me at his office door and motioned for me to sit in the chair in front of his desk as he took his oversized chair behind it. He sat there and just looked at me for a few moments as if he wasn't sure exactly how to proceed. Then he threw me a curve ball saying, "What are you going to do next year?"

Being just before Christmas, I assumed he meant in January after he had fired me. "Well," I said, "I own some apartments and a small construction company, so I will go back and build some more apartments."

With that, he sat back and looked at me some more. I wanted to say, *"Come on; let's get on with this. Fire me and get it over with."*

Instead, I waited, and he finally said, "If you could do anything you wanted to do with a classroom of kids, what would you do?"

I didn't know where he was going with that question, but it didn't sound too promising since I just wanted to go home for dinner. But, I assumed he was talking about my unorthodox approach to teaching and he was curious just how weird I would get if I had the chance.

Tentatively I said, "You mean with a class?" He nodded, and I jumped in with both feet; at least, I would get in a few jabs on the way out the door. My old grade school memories were flooding back again. I had a lot of heat built up around the topic of teachers, schools, and how they operated, and what it did to some kids. I let the superintendent have it with both barrels. For the next twenty-five to thirty minutes, I went on about all the things I believed kids could be doing, indeed, should be doing, in school instead of what they were doing now. There was no stopping me.

The superintendent sat through it with a bemused, enigmatic smile as I rolled out all my guns. I had waited a long time to tell a teacher-type, what side of the toast the butter was on, and I was going to make the most of it. I wasn't delivering my tirade to a teacher or even a principal; I had hooked a bigger fish, a superintendent.

He let me rant on, and when I finally stopped, he just sat there looking at me with that damned enigmatic smile. After a while, he quietly said, "You got it."

Then, it was my turn to sit there. I had no idea where this conversation was going, but it had definitely left me behind. "I got what?" I asked in surprise.

The Superintendent looked at me as though he were a patient man, dealing with a slow child, and said, "If you come back next year, you can have a class of kids and do with them, all of that."

I looked for flecks of foam around the man's mouth. Nothing he said made any sense as I was scrambling to get a handle on where this conversation had gone.

I guess he could see the bewilderment on my face. So he said, "If you will finish this year and come back next fall, you can have a class of kids you can work with in any way you want." Then he went on to say, "But there is a caveat; most of the kids you get will be ones who are bored or failing. In many cases, you'll get the three children out of each of the fourth, fifth, and sixth–grade classrooms who need something different. Some may be bright but bored, some will be troublemakers, and some are just kids the teachers have given up on. However, this way, the other teachers won't care what you do with them in your class, and it will keep the principal off your back."

That afternoon, instead of getting the ax, I met a person who would change the direction of my life once again, placing me exactly where some higher part wanted me to be. Nevertheless, I had no idea that what I had just signed on for, was for the rest of my life. Or, that its influence on my life would last long after I left teaching. Here was a man giving me a chance to prove what I thought schools could be, instead of what they had been for me. I now wondered if I could really help kids who struggled as I had. Was it really possible that most rebels and renegades were actually just dyslexics, ADDs, and ADHDs as I now suspected? Suddenly I wasn't so sure, now that I was faced with the reality of putting up or shutting up. But I felt that this man was also offering to help.

What we discovered during the next four years was gratifying and put what we both believed in a new light. We began to realize that every child who enters the first grade has far more abilities than schools realize, even those who fail in the first few grades. After all, they learned a foreign language, without books, teachers or lesson plans before they came to school. Furthermore, scientists who study the learning process now realize that learning one's first language is one of the most challenging accomplishments undertaken in life. And, while the a second language is easier (because we already understand the concept of a language), most still find it daunting.

We found curiosity was the key to redirecting failing kids. In fact, by understanding how to use a child's natural God-given curiosity was the key to real learning. Using the child's interest, coupled with the natural talent and passion that is innate in every child, could change schools and produce a generation of children that would change the world.

During a trip back to the afterlife, I found out that what Henry and I had discovered, was answers to part of the problem schools face. Apparently, if education is to begin preparing our children for all the rapid change that was ahead, then schools must rethink how learning actually happens in children.

In addition, it was explained that writing about those experiences was the way I would learn to write, myself. And, if I was to live up to the purpose for which I was sent back, to tell my story, I needed to learn to write.

However, I was also told that I first I had to learn the language of Inner Guidance, as it was a necessary part of the writing I was to do. So, I realized it would be a while before I would be ready to write anything.

I guess it was then that I began to understand how long I would be back here on Earth. But, eventually with lots of help from two Soul Guides who were about to show up, I wrote the two books about the experimental program Henry and I developed. They were Renegade Teacher and Renegade Class.

Renegade Teacher is the story of what the children did in the classroom during the five years Henry and I built and ran the program. Then, Renegade Class tells what became of those same children during the 40 years after leaving the program.

However, it was not meant for Henry and I to continue our journey together. A community to the north hired Henry to start a Community College based on the same principles we believed in. He invited me to help. However, that would have meant uprooting my family and taking the girls out of their school. Instead, something else was calling.

So, I left education, staying in our beloved Ashland, continuing to build apartments and migrating into building offices and commercial lease space. During the next few 15 years the financial success that I had dreamed of during my childhood materialized.

When I left education I had no way of knowing my tenure as a teacher, working with kids who struggled in school, was part of a role I had chosen for this life, lifetimes ago. Furthermore, it would come back into my life later, in an unusual way. Nor could I imagine that my success would become seemingly meaningless, as I came up against something that made money meaningless.

Chapter 14

Learning About Grief

Grief that surrounding death may pale in comparison to the grief of coming back from death.

June 1982

Once my mind accepted that I was returning to my old life, there was a soul-shaking jolt. Suddenly, I was suddenly back in my in my office, in my body, desperately clawing at my throat as I struggled to breathe.

After getting a few gulps of air, devastating grief flooded through my being replacing the joy, euphoria, and bliss I had experienced just moments before. Suddenly, I was back in my old earthly reality, once again. However, now I was left with waves of celestial memories, tantalizingly close, but just beyond reach. As with a fading dream, I felt that other reality, moving further and further away, but remaining hauntingly clear.

I had left the place of purest, profound love only to be hurtled back into the same sad old world full of loss, suffering and fear that I had left earlier. Now, the difference was that, someway, I knew that I had created my world with my old beliefs, which just made it all worse.

I'm not sure how long I sobbed inconsolably in my grief, but eventually my wife came rushing downstairs, fearing something tragic had happened. As I struggled to tell her, it brought all the pain of separation back as I sat there, choking on deep wracking sobs. Gently, she took my hand, and, with a look of deep caring concern, put her arm around me and just held me. She seemed to realize it was something about me and that there hadn't been a death in the family. Then, she quietly said, "I'm not sure what happened, but it must have been profound." Then we just sat there for a long while in comforting silence.

What happened over the next few days is a blur. Every time my mind went back to where I had been, waves of grief consumed me. I had no interest anymore in anything down here, but I knew I was here for a long time to come. For a number of days, I alternated between anger and despair. Nothing seemed to ease the pain, and I couldn't see how anything ever could, except my going home again.

I would have considered suicide but, somehow, I knew that was not an option anymore. I had already been there and accepted an assignment that precluded going back anytime soon.

While I was trying to deal with the loss of being back here, I also had to deal with something else that made it worse. I had also lost the many deeply-held personal beliefs that I used to make sense of life here on earth. Prior to my death, I was comfortable with the general belief that after death, oblivion ended it all forever. As long as I believed that, all I had to worry about, was winning the game, and nothing after death mattered, right?

Now all that changed, and I didn't have that comfort, and I didn't know what the rest meant. Prior to my NDE, one of the tenets I loosely subscribed to was one that was commonly held by many young American males: "He who has the most toys when he dies wins." According to that, I had been doing pretty well. But now, I realized that none of that mattered at all, and most of the things I had accumulated meant nothing. Along with that belief, went my standing and place within the crazy world in which I was now living.

Now, without a belief structure, my world, and its dramas was as empty and meaningless as the proverbial tinkling brass as in the old Sunday school Bible story. Where did that leave me? Without my old belief structure and not having yet assimilated a new one, I was left with nothing. What I had learned in Sunday school was far, far short of the mark and of no help. Worst of all, while I was "over there," I had been given nothing with which to replace my earthly beliefs, other than to know I would eventually go back.

However, now I had no idea how to play this new/old earthly game. All I really had was the promise that a new handbook was on the way.

Chapter 15

The Book That Found Me

That in which a gift is wrapped
does not belie its value

Late 1982

One day, while I was still lost between worlds, I was in Medford, north of Ashland. It followed weeks of wandering around, searching for something, exactly what I didn't know.

That day, I had found myself in front of a bookstore I hadn't seen before, and almost without thinking, I entered. Almost unaware of where I was, I began wandering among the shelves but quickly ran out of bookshelves. I browsed a few tables of books scattered about, but nothing caught my eye or even looked remotely interesting.

I didn't even know why I was in this town, let alone this store. I hadn't started out to find a bookstore. I was just lost again, feeling sorry for myself for agreeing to come back here at all. So, when I had stumbled across this little bookstore, I vaguely remembered being told that my Guides would be sending a user's guide, my instruction manual.

Since my return, I had pondered the concept of just what Inner Guidance was, and I concluded I didn't know. I certainly didn't hear any voices, and I didn't know for sure what a hunch was. Was it the same as the proverbial "gut feeling"? All I ever heard from anywhere inside was a bunch of mind-chatter, something I had heard all my life, and I didn't think for a moment that there was anything inspired about it. Most of it was just drivel. So, what was this Inner Guidance and how did one learn anything about it, let alone develop it into a dependable source of information and guidance?

Still pondering all this, I headed for the door. Just as I reached for the knob, a pleasant voice said, "Aren't you Duane Smith?" Now, that was a voice I could plainly understand, but I didn't think it came from within.

Surprised and not recognizing the voice, I turned and found a middle-aged woman sitting in a small alcove at a cluttered desk. Somewhat surprised that anyone here knew my name, I answered, "Yes, I'm Duane Smith."

She went on to say, "Your daughter Traci ordered a book from me; now that it has arrived, I can't seem to reach her. Is she possibly out of town?"

"No, I saw her this morning, so I know she's around. Look, why don't I just pay you for the book, and take it to her myself." So I paid her and left the store with Traci's book in a small paper bag, not thinking too much about it, not even thinking to ask how she knew I was Traci's dad.

On the drive back to Ashland, I passed a small park that caught my eye. One old Elm tree in particular was almost calling my name, inviting me to sit in its shade and read for awhile. I remember musing to myself, wondering if that tree was a form of inner or outer guidance.

Stopping the car, I reached for my "back-up" book, one I always kept with me for times when such urges came over me. I was partial to leisurely reading breaks in the shade of any tree, but that tree had called before. As I was getting out of the car, for some reason I also reached back for the little bag that held Traci's book. I guess I was curious about what she was reading these days, and, as I sat down, I took a small white book from the bag. Its title was *The Impersonal Life*, and where the author's name usually was, it just read Anonymous. Curious, I began to read.

Three hours later, I was still deeply engrossed in what was a rather fascinating little book. It was also all I read that night and the next day. For three weeks, it was all I read. I had my nose in that book, night and day. At the end of the three weeks, I was only six or eight pages into the first chapter.

It was a most unusual book. It had the most complex, unending sentences I had ever seen. Some were more than a page in length but correctly structured with proper syntax. They were incredibly hard to unwind, sort out, and comprehend. In retrospect, I now realize that the structure served a purpose that I did not grasp at the time, and each word, in its obtuse way, was absolutely compelling. I guess when you are thirsty enough you'll take water in any way you can get it, even if it is a drop at a time. Furthermore, it was the sweetest water I had ever tasted.

The book was unusual in several ways. After I spent several evenings, reading it, I happened to turn to the title page. The author was still listed as anonymous, and no place in the book could I get a clue as to who wrote it.

As time went on, I found *that* wasn't the only strange thing about this book. It was, in fact, a virtual fountain of knowledge about the still small voice and its seemingly various languages and dialects as well as what to listen for and how to sensitize oneself to it. However, no one but a determined, thirsty person would ever persevere long enough to grasp its obtuse meaning, page after page. I had read once that the ancient mystery schools taught that the world's greatest secrets were "hidden in plain sight." I now knew what that meant.

However, after a month or so, I had a feeling that I had kidnaped Traci's book. I was so caught up in it, that I had failed to mention it to her. So one morning, I went to her apartment and sheepishly explained what I had and where I had gotten it.

As I handed her the now well-worn copy, she looked at me with a puzzled look on her face and said, "Dad, I have never been in that bookstore in my life. I know what bookstore you're talking about; it's below 'Maggie's on Main,' one of the stores where I occasionally shop. However, I have never been inside it." Now I was the one puzzled.

Traci began scanning through the book. After a minute or so, she looked up and said, "Dad, this isn't my book. It doesn't speak to me at all. I would never have ordered this. Then she said something I didn't think much about until later. She said, "Dad, this must be your book."

On the way home, I pondered what I was told during my NDE, about the book that would find me. When I considered just how this book had gotten into my hands, there was little doubt that this book found me. I certainly hadn't found it.

There had been so many random events that all had to line up for me to be in that store. I wasn't even sure why I had even gone to that town, of all places I could have gone. What part did Inner Guidance play in my having this book, and how did it work? I still didn't have any idea. After all, what good was Inner Guidance if you're not aware of it? However, someway, it had it brought me to the right book and, someway, without knowing it, I found the right wife, across an ocean, in the midst of 60 million people?

In the weeks that followed, an important turning point in my life would manifest itself in a similar fashion.

Chapter 16

Life Becomes Bearable

*The dark just before the dawn makes us wonder
if the dawn will ever come.*

1982- 1984

As I began to settle into my new role in life, I often slept eighteen to twenty hours a day. Either I had a lot of catching up to do or it was something else. My mortal mind suddenly had a lot of information to process and absorb. It was information that I had been helped to re-remember, during my NDE, but would be available to me in my new role as I needed it.

At the time, I was also having vivid dreams that were unlike any dreams I had ever experienced. Sometimes, I could recall them, but most of the time, they danced just beyond reach. I had the feeling that they were still within recall, but they weren't, and they usually faded away into nothingness as I awoke. But for some reason it seemed important to capture them.

Later, I learned that only small parts of what was reawakened in my mind would be immediately available for my use, and not to concern myself with what wasn't. Instead, I was to remember who I really was, focus on what was immediately in front of me and enjoy the adventure. If I did that, I was assured the rest would fall into place, and new information would be available *when I needed it*.

During this period, I also began to realize I did not want to return to this life, after my NDE, for a different reason that I thought. At the time, I believed the world was a wretched place, and I just wanted to be somewhere else. Now I was beginning to realize that this might not be the case at all. Maybe the problem was how I was perceiving my world. Perhaps what I believed about the world, was wrong. I had been told that the world appeared to be, whatever we believed it to be. And, I was still having trouble with that concept.

However, what if that was right? What if we experience life just as we believe it to be? After all, where had I gotten my beliefs about what the world was like; My parents; people around me; the Media? What if it was all wrong?

One of the reasons that made any sense at all was what I learned about Heaven. After my first trip to the other side, I came to realized that people first experience heaven, just as they expect it to be, from whatever beliefs they had about it before the died. *(Which is why heaven is described*

88

differently by the different people who have Afterlife experiences.)

The Afterlife, even though I didn't believe in God when I died, was like what I had learned from my short tenure in Sunday school, and maybe from an old movie or two. I did seem to have some degree of an expectation when I arrived. And yes, it lived up to that small expectation and surpassed it beyond measure.

So, when I was told that life here on Earth, conforms to our beliefs, not the other way around, I began to question one of my basic assumptions. Was it possible that I saw what I believed, instead of believing what I saw? When I began to grasp that, I realized that, if that were so, by changing my beliefs, I could change my world.

Had I realized that earlier I could have *believed* that my sleep apnea was curable, would it have been, as it was years later? But, had that been so, I would not have had my NDE. Was it possible that the original cause of my sleep apnea was just a deep-seated subconscious belief that, in some way had served me well? After all, it was the cause of my NDE and what I was now experiencing. Was that the reason why the autonomic nervous system conveniently "forgot" to tell my body to breathe? If so, did I write that script myself?

That thought made me wonder. If that was correct, just who was running my show? I had thought my mortal mind was, but so much had happened that was beyond my control, it made me wonder.

At the time, after my NDE, my primary sleep care physician fitted me with something called a C-Pap Machine, which allowed me to breathe and sleep at the same time. In the process, he assured me that he had never heard or seen anyone cured of central nervous sleep apnea unless you consider death a cure.

However, in my case, after wearing out four different C-Pap machines, my sleep apnea faded into nothingness. Now, thirty years after I was first fitted with it, I no longer display any symptoms and no longer need the machine. I am no longer seeing that doctor, which worked out perfectly as well. His reality is still intact and conforms to his belief structure. He probably still assures anyone who asks, that there is no cure for central nervous system sleep apnea. And that is as it should be.

In time, I have found that we will always reject anything that doesn't fit our current belief structure, *until* we are ready to question that original belief. After all, *why would we be interested in something that contradicts the truth as we see it?* Furthermore, we rarely question our beliefs unless something causes at least a partial paradigm shift.

Since my doctor is very invested in his current medical model, he could not accept my story anyway. Before he could do that, he would need a larger shakeup in his whole belief structure. One story by some crackpot who claims he had an NDE wasn't going to do that. My story might only serve to entrench him even further. If he were really to question his current belief structure around medicine, he would be forced to define a whole medical model, causing him to redefine his role in life.

Of course, one of the major benefits of my NDE was that it thoroughly shattered most of my belief structure, leaving me open to a new reality. Without it, I would have remained stuck in my old paradigm. However, until that promised book arrived, I was at a loss to know how to start rebuilding.

Chapter 17

The Mystery Deepens

Mystery creates wonder and wonder is the basis of man's need to understand.

Morgan Cottle, circa 2014

Late 1982

Had it been anyone else other than my eldest daughter, who said she hadn't been in that bookstore, let alone ordered the book, I would have put it down to a forgotten moment. But over the years, I had learned that when Traci said something like that, you could take it to the bank. She was uncannily accurate about such matters, just like her mother and sister. I used to say it was their German heritage. I had learned long ago never to argue with them when they said they had done something or hadn't done something.

So that evening, I left my daughter's house with my new book, now a well-worn book, one that never stopped speaking to me, and one that I would never finish. As time went on, I found it to be a never-ending source of knowledge and inspiration, not because it contained everything I needed to know but because it helped tap the endless esoteric knowledge from within. As Frank and Amos had explained, the words in a book, even the Bible, are meaningless. Words have no meaning in themselves. They only have the meaning that we attach to them. This is the reason why so many different people can read the same thing and have it mean entirely entire different things.

This human quirk destroys friendships and is the cause of many wars. I now understand that the words in and of themselves, are meaningless. It is the meaning our intellect applies to a word, that reflects back to use, the meaning then applies to it. But the brain only knows the meanings it has learned from its environment, and often what we have learned is wrong.

However, it is the interpretation that the Still Small Voice can apply that will bring the truth from within. It is also why *The Impersonal Life*, continures to provide new information over the years, as I grow more comfortable with it's use.

However, if there were within me an all-wise, all-knowing part, an infallible source of information, I wanted to know how to be able to communicate with it. And, most importantly, I needed to know what language it spoke so I wasn't fooled by the voice of the ego instead.

As the years went by, I found just how different this book was and how much energy the universe (read: God Matrix) invested in putting the right book in my hands at the right time. Once I knew and stated my desire, for my will to be God's will for me, the details started taking care of themselves. It seemed to be a process, not instantaneous, in my case, at least.

After I had read that book two, three, or, sometimes, four hours a day for a year or two, the pages started falling out. In time, *The Impersonal Life* became a stack of loose pages, instead of a neatly bound little white book, and I decided it was time to buy a new copy. For this reason, the next time I was downtown, I went to The Golden Mean Bookstore, the only purely metaphysical bookstore in Ashland at the time.

I didn't find a copy on the shelves, so I went to the owner. When I told her the name of the book, I could see it didn't register with her. She asked me if I knew the publisher's name. When I told her, she pulled a couple of catalogs off a shelf by her desk. After a few minutes of looking at various publishers catalogs, she said, "I can't find such a book listed; are you sure of the title and publisher?"

When I said that I was sure and that I had bought a copy of it a year ago in Medford, she looked at me for a moment and said, "I don't know about that, but I just went back into that publisher's catalogues, and they have had nothing in print, by that name, in the last seven years."

The next morning, after spending an hour with my little stack of pages, I confirmed the publisher. I got in my car and headed to Northern California. After all, when a person is dying of thirst, running out of water is not an option, and water is wherever you can find it. So, I headed for the little town of Mount Shasta City, California, about an hour's drive south of Ashland on Interstate 5. Over the years, Mt. Shasta had attracted seekers of various kinds, and I had heard that there was an incredible metaphysical bookstore there. I had wanted to peruse its shelves for several years, so today was as good a time as any.

An hour and a half later, I was up to my neck in metaphysical books, new and old. However, even after several hours of combing the shelves, I was again empty-handed. I had already spoken to the owner, and she hadn't found it in her catalogs either. I was growing more and more puzzled.

As I was leaving, the owner stopped me and said, "I've been thinking; there's a small metaphysical bookstore on a ranch about twelve miles west of town. You might check with the owner. She has some old and very unusual books. I often find something with her that I can't find anywhere else."

So, I headed out into the ranchland west of Mount Shasta. For some reason, as I drove, I felt almost euphoric. I put the feeling down to being in the shadow of a high mountain that reminded me of the Alps of Europe, or maybe the Himalayas of Tibet, with its echoes of past lives. I certainly could understand why Shasta had such an effect on people. I didn't know if it had any special "aura" or metaphysical significance, as many here believed, but I surely liked being in its shadow. Or maybe it was something else entirely. If I could find another copy of the book, possibly it might contain a clue to its origin.

Chapter 18

A Stranger in a Strange Land

It's been said that being lost is a state of mind. One always knows where they are; it's the rest of the world they've lost.

The End of 1982

It was a confusing time. On one hand, I had some unusual experiences. And, in some ways, I felt like I had been given the keys to the Kingdom. But, on the other hand, I was losing everything that I had cherished and was dear to me. My only consolation was that now I had a book in my hands that seemed to validate what had happened, and promised to be a jumping off point for a new way of living life.

I tried to correlate my situation with something to which I could relate. It occurred to me that I was much like the man in a fable of my childhood.

"Once upon a time, there was a poverty-stricken old man who thought himself a bit of a philosopher and went about extolling his wisdom. Unfortunately, no one paid him any heed, and he was reduced to living in a wretched ghetto, combing garbage bins for something to eat.

One day, while digging in a mound of garbage, he came across an old pot of some sort. He started to throw it aside, but, without thinking, he rubbed it with his shirt sleeve, wondering what was under the grime.

Suddenly, in a puff of smoke, a genie appeared. Soon, there was the customary exchange between a genie and his apparent new master, and the old vagrant found himself being transported to the city of his dreams, Paris.

Once in Paris, with his newfound great wealth, he was soon held in great esteem as a philosopher. He lived in a grand villa, in the best part of Paris, just off the Place de la Concorde. Soon, he was delivering his pearls of wisdom in lectures to packed crowds among the intelligentsia of the University. He was the toast of society, always surrounded by friends and loved ones. Without saying, the old vagrant enjoyed his new life, as he fulfilled his every indulgence and whim.

Then one fine day, he suddenly found himself on the way back to his old ghetto, broke and unable to speak French or now, even his native tongue. When he got there, he was lost. Not knowing what else to do, he made his way to his old hovel, only to find a new building standing where he once lived.

As he stood there dazed, his genie appeared once more and said, "Sorry pal, your time was up." Then, noticing the old man's wretched condition, said, "Hey pal, I'll send along a few of your old school books as you will need to learn to speak your native language again. But, you'll be fine, so don't worry. In fact, you're gonna' love it!" And with that, he was gone.

That was the way I felt—utterly hopeless, destitute and lost. In addition, I now felt a far greater despair than when I had known I was dying. Now, I saw no end in sight unless this new book was going to change it all, but I couldn't see how it could.

As you can imagine, those around me sensed my dismay at being back and didn't quite know what to make of it. Some just thought I had been "playing football without my helmet on," as one person said. As for my wife, I can only imagine the rejection she must have felt, and I had no way of explaining that it wasn't about her. Someday, we both would understand, but maybe not in this life.

As for my girls, to this day, I am not sure what they thought. Luckily, they were in high school and absorbed in boyfriends and teen culture, and it seemed to lessen the impact. However, probably for the rest of their lives, they will watch their father out of the corner of their eye for any sort of strange behavior.

As days turned into weeks, the self-pity seemed to wear itself out, as I delved deeper into my magical little white book. Slowly I began to question whether the problems with the world might not be as I had thought them to be. Paragraph by obscure paragraph, another reality started to gradually take hold of my mind, a little corner here and a little corner there. Perhaps all that had happened wasn't about my dying or returning. Could it possibly be about something larger?

Chapter 19

Was it a Dream

Over the years, people have asked if my experience could possibly have been a dream. Frankly, if someone else had told me a similar story, before my NDE, I might well have asked the same question. However, please consider a Native American is encountering a similar out-of-this-world experience in another time.

"Imagine if you will, that 180 years ago before settlers came west, you were a Native American with no knowledge of other races or people other than that of your own.

In time, your tribe began hearing wild tales of "a white devil," who lived far away and sometimes rode west in the belly of giant iron beast that ran like the wind across the prairie. Some even said that the beast puffed great clouds of fire and smoke from its nostrils, as it chased two shiny lines across the country. Living in a culture, as you did, where even the wheel was, as yet unknown, your people naturally thought such wild tales to be the stories of addled old people or the ranting of young braves from smoking too much loco weed.

Now, imagine if you can, that one morning, you are out on the prairie far from your village, following the tracks of a young buck. As you quietly creep up on your prey, you come across two curious, shiny lines in the grass, and your eyes follow them as they run off to the mountains in the distance.

Momentary distracted from your hunt, you lay your bow on a mossy boulder that's close by. Then, opening a leather pouch from a thong around your neck, you tear off a piece of dried venison to chew on as you sit pondering this curious trail.

Watching the sun's glint on the lines in the grass, you notice a small, rodent-like critter following the lines, far-off toward the mountains. Curiously, you watch it grow bigger and bigger as it comes your way.

Suddenly, right in front of your eyes, it turns into a raging black beast as your first steam-driven locomotive comes barreling down the tracks straight toward you.

As it roars past, a violent blast of hot steam and smoke knocks you off your mossy rock, and a thunderous roar overwhelms your senses. As it passes within an arm's length of where you're lying, you feel the blazing heat of its red-hot boiler on your face and the stench of black smoke searing your nose and throat. Your face and arms sting from burning embers as you hunker in fear on the ground.

When the beast is past, you finally gather your things and make your way back to the village, trying to make sense of what you saw. Finally, as you sit around the evening fire, you gather the courage to tell your story.

However, your telling meets skeptical ears, and your friends begin to avoid your eyes. When you are finished with your telling, it grows very still around the fire.

Finally, a wise old grandfather of the tribe softly says, "My young brave, it was the warm morning sun. It caused you to fall asleep, casting a spell on you, bringing such fanciful dreams."

As you listen, you see your friends nod their heads in acceptance of this explanation and quickly begin talking of the day's hunt. So, you just sit, watching the fire.

Later that night, as you lay under the buffalo robe, you wonder if the old grandfather was right. Could it have been just the sun and a dream?

But, the next morning you are up before the dawn, to return to the prairie; to look for the strange trail in the grass, to see if the smoke puffing dragon might appear today again.

Finally, after many days of sitting along the tracks, watching, once again the beast speeds by. Then, after many days of waiting and watching, the white devil stops the beast inviting you into its belly. At first, you're afraid, but, in time, after seeing that the white devil was just a man with white skin, you accept his offer and take a ride in the beast.

Soon, you're feeling the wind in your hair, as you too speed across the prairie, watching steam and fire pour from the nostrils of the great iron contraption. As you ride, you realize that, to your friends, the beast would always be a crazy dream, until the day they too take a ride in the beast. Until then, their opinion of the story does not change the reality of what you experienced. Having walked the same path they are walking now, you understand how they might question your story.

Today, if anyone asks me whether I could have been dreaming, I might well ask if they had read what the Apostle Paul said in his letter to the Corinthians, as recorded in I Corinthians 13:12. *"For now **we see through a glass darkly**, but **then, face to face.**"*

With that in mind, and with the deepest humility, I will now endeavor to tell the rest of my story, just as I experienced it and just as I was sent back to do. If some part of my truth resonates with some part of your truth, then take it with you, for this is as it should be.

If some part of my truth does not fit with all of your truth, consider it for a while, before leaving it, and take the part that resonates with your truth.

In addition, if some part of your truth violently disagrees with some part of my truth, that too, is as it should be. For, if you leave these pages knowing, for sure, that your truth is right for you, we both have served the purpose for which we were drawn together; to find our truth. To that end, may you find that which you were seeking when you picked up this book.

Chapter 20

The End of the Rainbow

Where a real pot of gold is revealed

Late 1983

After, not finding another copy of *The Impersonal Life* in the other bookstores in Mt. Shasta, I followed the directions to the bookstore I was told about. After several miles of traveling down a country road, I found a cozy little bungalow tucked under some tall pine trees, near a clutch of barns. Above a side door was a small sign, barely visible from the road that just said, "Books" with a little arrow. As I got out of the car, I could smell the pine trees, and there was a breathtaking view of the mountain. However, what held my attention was the cozy feeling that enveloped me like a warm blanket.

Above the door was a small, hand-lettered sign that simply read, "Come In," and I cautiously opened the door. As I stepped in a woman entered the room, almost as though she were expecting me. I don't remember what she looked like, but she was a friendly older woman, and I remember her wearing a purple, flowing dress.

After greeting me, she asked how she could help me, and I told her what I wanted. Then, with a bemused smile, and without moving from where she stood, she reached up and removed a little white book from a bookshelf next to her. In retrospect, what surprises me is that, at the time, I wasn't surprised at all. It seemed, so normal. After all, that is the way the world is supposed to work, isn't it?

I opened the cover, and there was a price of $2.00 neatly printed in the upper left-hand corner of the flyleaf. As I stood there, all I remember thinking was how the book felt so good in my hand. It was only later that I realized that I had paid $8.95 for my first copy.

I don't remember paying for the book or how long we talked. But I know we talked for a while. About what, I don't know. In addition, I have no memories of driving home that day, other than how I felt. At the time, I know the whole sequence of events didn't seem unusual. All that seemed important was that I had my book and that it felt good. By the time that second copy had worn out, *The Impersonal Life* was available in all the new catalogs and often was on the shelves of any decent metaphysical bookstore and on Amazon as an eBook.

Over the years, I have worn out six or eight more copies, and I've given away many more. However, it never has been and probably never will be a big seller. After all, there usually isn't much traffic on the road less traveled. However, we all must find our own particular book which speaks to us personally, from within, not from without. A book is only one method of Hearing the Inner Voice.

For me, the key to hearing the Inner Voice was *The Impersonal Life*, my key to my hearing and beginning to decipher the source of wisdom within. It was the book promised me during my NDE.

As soon as I began reading, I knew I was hearing was the Voice of Inner Knowledge and Wisdom, applying its own meaning to the words, as the Inner Voice read them to my mind and intellect. It was then I really understood that words are meaningless. Usually, we hear the meaning our intellect has learned to give those words. For example, the word "cup" it can mean many things to many people. There are big cups, little cups, grease cups, bra cups, tin cups, and porcelain tea cups; the list is endless. However, when we read the word "cup" in a story, we apply the meaning our intellect elects to come up with this time, nothing more. Furthermore, it is usually done without thinking.

As I read the first page, suddenly a whole new world began to blossom forth from within. Here is what I heard my Inner Voice say that day, after a few hours of parsing.

To you who read, I speak.

To you, who, through long years and much running to and fro, have been eagerly seeking, in books and teachings, in philosophy and religion, for you know not what—Truth, Happiness, Freedom, God;

To you whose Soul is weary and discouraged and almost destitute of hope;

To you, who many times have obtained a glimpse of that "Truth" only to find, when you followed and tried to reach it, that it disappeared in the beyond and was but the mirage of the desert;

To you, who thought you had found it in some great teacher, who was perhaps the acknowledged head of some Society, Fraternity or Religion, and who appeared to you to be a "Master," so marvelous was the wisdom he taught and the works he performed; —only to awaken later to the realization that that "Master" was but a human personality, with faults and weaknesses, and secret sins, the same as you, even though that personality may have been a channel through which were voiced many beautiful teachings, which seemed to you the highest "Truth;"

And here you are, Soul aweary and enhungered, and not knowing where to turn—To you, I am come.

Finally, the universe had given me an entry-level key, what I did with it was now up to me.

Later, I also realized it was just the first of several assignments that I would be given, each to teach me to hear and understand the many levels of that which had been inside me all along.

But at the time, little did I know that the assignments would become more obscure, as obtuse sentences distracted my mortal mind, allowing Inner Voice to shine through to the Intellect. It was not unlike the matter of locating *The Impersonal Life*, little was expected of me, as my mortal mind was distracted by the hunt. Other than that, I had just gone along for the ride, so to speak. I was just put in the right place at the right time. In the next assignment, more would be asked of me. I would need to learn to understand Guidance from Within at an ever-higher level. And. Without realizing I had started on a journey that was to last the rest of this life and beyond, forever applying new meaning to the expression, "it's the journey, not the destination."

Chapter 21

Taken Back Again

In which I feel that old going home feeling again

Early 1984

One rainy afternoon just after I had recovered my book again, I found myself falling through space again. This time was different. It wasn't a near-death experience but an out-of-body (OOB) experience. After a few moments, I knew what was happening and where I was going. The same warm sensation rose from my lower chakra, and, once again, blossomed slowly upward through my entire being, filling me with an ecstasy as desirable as pure love itself. I was on my way back once more. I was going home again. I knew it was only a visit, but a visit as anticipated and longed for as any visit home ever was.

This time, shortly after I separated from my body back on earth, two entities were there to greet me. Once again, a feeling of deep, infinite love surrounded me, and, again, that old "coming-home feeling" overpowered my senses. If my eyes could have cried, they would have been streaming tears.

I soon learned from these entities were part of my old Soul Group, and that they would be my Guides for a series of return trips and, indeed, had been my Guides while I was on earth prior to my NDE. However, for some reason, while they seemed familiar, I didn't recognize them right away.

As we traveled toward our destination, they told me with no a little amusement, that as my earlier Soul Guides on earth, they found me to be a challenge to deal with. Apparently I hadn't paid much attention to them during the last few decades. They said it seemed to take more and more, to get my attention as time went on. Then, when even a severe medical condition didn't work, they had decided to go with another plan.

Apparently, they had bailed me out on a number of occasions, getting me out of jams and scrapes I had gotten myself into, which I later claimed credit for myself. They relayed this to me without the least sense of judgment, and their loving presence dispelled any of the anxiety I might have, otherwise, felt.

Soon, we stopped at a little oasis that had miraculously appeared, just as if we were stopping at a rest stop along the interstate. Then, as we lounged there, they began retelling some of the messes I had gotten into, and it seemed to amuse them a great deal. In fact, I couldn't help but stop and stare at one of them, as he had a bemused, wry smile that seemed so familiar.

"Do I remind you of someone?" he finally said with a twinkle in his eye.

To which I curiously replied, "I'm not sure. Should you?"

"Then, think back; if I do remind you of someone, who would it be?

"Well, your smile reminds me of one of my granddads when I was a boy."

"Really now, and who also in your past, does that other guy bring to mind, gesturing to the other entity who was watching.

Now, I looked over at him. It was as if the picture just came into focus. There stood Amos from my days as a lad on the farm in the Applegate, my pal and buddy from the mill. Then, as I turned back, there stood Grandpa Frank, with that bemused wry smile, the smile I had seen so many times as a boy so many years ago.

As we stood there, off somewhere in a little corner of the cosmos, it all came flooding back. There were all the golden memories of a magical boyhood before my life took what, at the time, seemed to be a turn for the worse. Now I wasn't sure whether it was a turn for the worse or not. Here I was with two of my favorite people/entities as my Soul Guides, a role they had apparently played all along.

117

A thousand questions flooded my mind. But before I could ask the first, Amos suggested we get started on my agenda for this trip. "After all," he said, "you have another earthly guide waiting for a response from you on a job he has for you.

Chapter 22

Frank and Amos Again

Home is where the heart is.

—Pliny the Elder

Early 1984

This trip to the Afterlife was entirely different from the first. In fact, it was more of a magical sojourn through the cosmos with Frank and Amos, with a little history and a lot of philosophy thrown in. This time, other than their putting on a physical appearance for me, it was all nonphysical. This time, there were no buildings, no beautiful lawns and gardens, no physical anything. And by now, even Frank, Amos nor I had a physical appearance.

When I commented on this, Amos said, "Initially, as you know, on one's first trip to heaven after each incarnation, we always allow you to project heaven in a physical way, in almost any way you wish. After all, there is no set way heaven is or has to be. It's more of a state of mind than anything else. And, since it is a place to regroup and enjoy your time between lifetimes and other adventures, you are meant to be happy while you are there. So, why not let you project it any way you wish?"

Frank continued, "This is done only to make 'newbies' cofortable. We want heaven to be exactly as they expect it to be, so they feel as comfortable and 'at home', as possible."

Then Amos added, "Some people want it in the physical for a long time. Others don't seem to care once they get the idea of heaven being a state of mind and not a physical place. After that, it's up to each soul how they want to experience heaven."

Then Frank added, "And that, of course, is the reason why reports from first-time NDEers, differ so widely. Their first visits vary as widely as their beliefs. And, if you ask any human what they believe heaven is like, you will get all kinds of answers to that question. Furthermore, that is the kind of heaven they will experience, at first anyway.

This brought up something for me, so I asked, "If heaven is nonphysical, why does it seem so far away?"

The answer surprised me when Frank said, "Heaven seems far away because you think it is. Actually, as you have heard before, heaven isn't a place at all; it's a state of mind, and it isn't dependent on where you are. Some people experience heaven on earth most of the time, some never.

Here Amos picked it up. "Listen, I know you have already heard all this, but it will take a while for it to soak in. The mortal mind has will have to re-stack its whole deck of cards. But don't worry; it will sort itself out sooner than you think. And, what's the hurry? You have an eternity."

The idea of heaven as you expect it to be, brought up another question, or idea. "Wait," I said, "let me guess. That means hell is real after all, and it too will be just as we expect it to be, right? And, it's also a state of mind that can be experienced anywhere we are. Am I right?

"Bingo!" Amos replied, "Just look around when you get back to the physical. Then, try to tell me that some humans aren't living in a hell as scary as that guy Dante ever dreamed up."

"Well," I said, "when I wasn't taken to hell for, not believing in God when I died, I began to wonder if there really was such a place."

"Don't fool yourself," Amos replied. "Remember, humans have free will and the mortal mind, with its fear, can dream up some pretty scary scenarios. If you become a soul guide someday, you will find that most of your time is spent trying to get the attention of some of your charges who are in absolutely hellish situations. Occasionally, you may even have to step in and save their bacon. However, don't expect to get any credit for it."

"It's the free will that gets us in trouble isn't it?" I asked.

"Bingo!" said Amos. "Humans keep thinking their limited monkey mind can figure a way out of all their problems. But, fat chance. A mind that "thinks" its way into a problem can never think its way out."

And that's quite sad, too," added Frank, "because it's so simple once they take the hint. But, man's beliefs and fears, keep him blind and chained in the dark. And, as some wise human once said, *there are none so deaf as those who won't hear and none so blind as those who won't see.*"

I knew that it would be some time until I sorted all that out, but I was still curious about one aspect of human suffering. So I asked, "I can understand that much of people's suffering is self-imposed, but what about sickness? That doesn't seem self-imposed."

Frank took that one and said, "At some level, everything is self-imposed from poor choices. But overtly, most sickness is really just a wake-up call. After all, if the divine part of every person is God, and God can do anything, he can heal the body he shares with his mortal part, don't you think?"

So, I asked, "Why would God allow their body to be sick to begin with?"

"Ah," he went on, "there is a divine purpose to sickness. That purpose is to say,'Hey, wake up, you mortal part of me. I'm right here, as close as your breath. Use your free will to ask for help; once you learn my language, I will take care of all your problems."

I was beginning to get the idea. "Okay, so if they don't listen, they just get sicker, right? If they still don't listen, then they eventually will change, even if it's their last breath, as in my case, right?"

"Wrong," they both chimed in.

"Not quite," said Amos with a chuckle. "In your case, you had to go kicking and screaming all the way. Kiddo, you didn't have a clue until you arrived at the pearly gates!"

Chagrined, I said, "I guess I'm just a slow learner."

"No, just tenacious," Frank put in. "That's one of the reasons you fit your earthly role so well. And tenacious is an asset, once you get the Inner Guidance part, down pat." Then he went on, "We are going to focus on that part of your training first, as soon as you get back on Earth. Then, with what we have planned, we think you'll do fine."

"We have some challenging assignments for you, once you can begin to understand Inner Guidance. On this side, we are helpless unless you can communicate with us," added Amos.

"How will I ever know where to begin?" I asked.

"Don't worry about that part. How did you find your little book we sent you?" asked Frank. "We were pushing and nudging and yelling, but you were as unaware as a fat trout that is already full of worms. You were so busy trying to hear that you were deaf. Finally, you almost gave up and stopped trying so hard. And, that my friend was when we began to get through to you. Then, once you stumbled into that bookstore, it got easier. It is a little like the golfer praying to God for the strength, to hit the ball easy."

"Remember," said Frank, "part of your early lessons will be about learning to listen to your Inner Voice. And I can tell you, your mortal mind won't be of any help in this. In fact, it isn't capable of doing what we will be asking you to do. In addition, it won't want to lose the control and will resist you in any way it can."

One of the first things we'll have you learn is how to shut off the chatter of the monkey mind. As long as it has free run of your thinking, you are in trouble. In fact, it still thinks that if you just do what it tells you, it can set everything right." Then he added, "But, don't you believe it for a minute. If you are ever tempted to listen to that monkey mind of yours, just think of all the problems it got you into in the past."

Amos then said, "Frank, let's see if Duane has learned anything. Let's see if he can put any of his studies and what you just said, to use on the way home, with our help, of course. Now that he knows Heaven is a state of mind, maybe we won't have so far to travel on the way back."

"Or maybe farther," Frank observed with that bemused, wry smile I had known so well, so long.

Chapter 23

To Hell and Back

If you don't believe in hell,
just watch the evening news.

1984

As Frank and Amos ended the theoretical part of this trip's lesson, we began the practical part. For this, I realized I would be getting some hands-on experience, if you will, in Celestial navigation; in returning to the same point in time, as well as same point in the universe that I had left.

Before we began, they gave me some instruction on basic protection, in case my amateur attempts at celestial navigation failed. It was during this explanation that I realized they had something up their sleeves. Frank led off, innocently enough, by returning to the subject of hell. Once on the topic, he said, "To really understand hell, you first need to know that everything in the celestial realm is always subject to the will of God. Remember that, and it makes everything easier and not so scary." Then, turning to Amos, he said, "You do a better job of explaining the reasoning behind hell than I do. Can you explain that?"

Without missing a beat, Amos picked it up. "At the time of the creation, God wanted to provide choice and diversity, so he added a sprinkling of negative forces to the mix of positive. Thankfully, these positive forces outweighed the negative, and that is important to remember. You are always safe, no matter what, *as long as you remember who you are,* and a few other basics."

He then went on. "I can't stress enough that these negative forces, which you call evil, always remain subject to God's will. They are only souls exercising their free will while providing the full range of choices in the karmic adventures that you chose. In a sense, they provide the spice in the dramas you came here to enjoy. —"

"I don't get it," I interjected. "Why would we choose to mess with anything evil? Isn't that always risky or dangerous?"

"Well, certainly it is; that's the point," said Frank. "Let me ask you something. You enjoy playing poker, don't you?"

"Sure," I replied.

"Well, if you went to a game where the dealer always dealt everyone a perfect hand, how long do you think you would stay in the game?" asked Frank.

"Well, that wouldn't be a game at all," I said.

"Right", Amos interjected, "and would you pay eight or ten dollars to ride a roller coaster going in circles on the ground?"

"Of course not," I said in a quieter voice, beginning to get his drift.

"We all love adventure," he went on. "How long would you enjoy heaven if you really did just sit around on white fluffy clouds, playing a harp and singing for eternity?"

"Not very long," was my resolute reply.

Here, Frank interjected, "You see, we are all creative, vibrant souls, and we abhor sameness. We enjoy the new and different."

Then Amos added, "God created diversity because eternity is a long time, and we all, as parts of God, will seek ways to be challenged and to grow and create. That was one reason you were attracted to the material universe, it's new and different, relatively speaking."

"We all love drama, and the material incarnation is full of it. However, we should remember that 'evil villain' who might well seek to terminate your life in your 'current drama' is just part of the excitement you signed on for. The Soul came here safe and will still be safe, when it is over."

"However, you needn't worry too much about that. Being terminated (read 'killed') doesn't actually turn out to be as terrible as some humans seem to think. Prior to leaving the Eternal, the Soul wrote it's current drama, knowing full-well that to make our current earth game meaningful, it would need to write in challenge, fear, and excitement. It also realized that it would need to forget who it really was and be very selective in what it could remember of it Celestial origins.

The entity who had been terminated, can then merrily go on its way to future adventures, or it can choose a riskier and possibly destructive route, by returning to inflict revenge on the other Entity that terminated its incarnation. Of course, if it does that, it risks starting a whole new cycle of negative Karma which can last lifetimes, until one or the other tires of it and moves on to begin cleaning up the mess.

"Well kid," that's about enough of that; enough talk don't you think?" interjected Frank. "Let's go get some real hands-on, practical experience, and maybe get a little excitement as well."

So next, they were soon showing me the basics of celestial navigation and how to hold in my mind a picture of my destination. Then we were off to give it a whirl.

This turned out to be not as simple as it appeared, and soon, due to my ineptitude, we stumbled into a few places that definitely weren't home. I got into a few alternate universes, as, I imagine they knew I would.

One of the alternate universes apparently had one less dimension than the earth. But it seemed vaguely familiar. Nevertheless, everything was running at odd angles. There were trains and automobiles, somewhat similar to what we have here, but they moved differently.

I was questioned about this later, by someone who said, they had researched the matter. It was their considered opinion that such a two-dimensional reality could not exist in a three-dimensional material universe. While his statement sounded plausible, I knew at the time, that what I was experiencing wasn't in the material universe at all. In fact, the material universe is a tiny percentage of God's Realm, and a recent creation. It helps if I remember that even this material universe is mostly a projection of the mind we share with God. And, now, even the latest in Quantum Physics hints at this.

The whole question is a bit like considering how long eternity is. It is impossible to fathom by someone anchored by lifetimes in the material universe. We have agreed to be too limited in the use of the all-knowing part of our mind, in order to make the experience here, realistic. Once again, as Paul said in his letter to the Corinthians, *"Now we see through a glass, darkly; but then face to face." 1 Corinthians 13:12.*

The alternate reality I saw was very similar to a book I read as a child about a two-dimensional world called Flatland. I can't help but believe that the author of that book, at some time, had experienced the alternate reality I had bumped into. Being an artist, he could illustrate a children's book that demonstrated what I experienced far better than I could in words. I soon found that it is very difficult to translate other realities with the limitation of language.

Undaunted by my first missteps with no apparent negative consequences, and prodded by Frank and Amos, we went back to the beginning and I became a little braver. After all, I had complete faith in my Guides.

However, on this attempt, I stumbled into a place of incarnate evil. There were thousands of evil entities, right out of central casting. And, they all wanted a piece of me as they snarled and hissed. Instantly, terror coursed through me as if I were in the worst nightmare I had ever experienced, and the stench nearly overpowered me.

I immediately forgot that Frank and Amos were with me as I started to panic. Then, I heard the calming voice of Frank saying, "Remember who you are and visualize the white light of God surrounding you. Now, remembering who you are, push them back with your light."

I thought of the white light I had seen in heaven and imagined it surrounding me. Then, as I pushed it out from me, instantly they shrunk back and then, snarling and hissing, began to retreat, throwing off the evilest smell imaginable.

At that point, they were no less evil than before, and even today, I can still smell the stench and hear their snarling as they retreated enough to let us through. Eventually, we were able to walk on through the snarling, hissing crowd, as a path opened up ahead of us and closed behind us as we left that place. I can only imagine what might have happened had it not been for the help of Frank and Amos.

Since I am still around to write about it, obviously I got us back. Actually, with much help from Frank and Amos, I eventually stumbled and bumped my way back to that little iridescent, blue sphere, on the far edge of the Milky Way, deep in a nondescript, minor solar system. Eventually, we arrived where I was headed, in my bed, in my home in Ashland, Oregon, at the same time I had departed.

Along the way, Frank said that any time I found myself in a dangerous situation, anywhere I happened to be in God's realm, including the physical universe, all I or anyone else, needed to do was what they had just shown me in hell. That is, to first just remember who we really are. Then, to surround ourselves with his light and love calling on the force to which all other forces in the universe are subject. Furthermore, whenever you call on God in this manner, they assured me, you'll always walk through *any* danger, untouched.

Finally, Frank observed, "By the time we arrived you seemed to be getting the hang of this Inner Guidance thing. Not that the path isn't a long one. Frank and I have been studying it for several lifetimes and we're still just novices in the art, so we all have a long time to go. However, we have all Eternity to get there, and you are off to a great start. And, I assure you that Frank and I look forward to our coming times together. We have a lot planned for you. You will be as busy as a cat on a hot tin roof. But remember, above all else, you main job is to work on Inner Guidance. All falls into place when you can, at will call on the force within, and it will make your coming journey, a lot easier and a whole lot more fun.

"And, it won't be all book-learning either," interjected Frank. We have plenty of projects and activities planned for you, plus a few more, out of this world trips on the agenda. You ain't seen nothing yet!

"You always liked to build things. Boy do we have an assignment ahead for you. But before that, we have something else which needs doing. And, I guarantee, both of these projects will give you plenty of chance to polish your Inner Guidance skills because they are things you don't know anything about. So, stay alert and maybe this time, we won't have to drop things on your head to get your attention. Then, both of them grew quiet and Frank said, "Don't worry; we won't be far away, and with that, they faded away.

The next evening while I sat reading the book Frank and Amos finally got to me, I was also reflecting on all that had happened. As I pondered it all, I couldn't help but wonder what I should be watching for next, and how long I would have to wait.

Be sure to read the preview chapter to the following book in this series, on the next page.

To receive a free White Papers about NDEs and to be notified when the next book in the series is available, go to www.duane@agnosticsNDE.com.

Preview of Book II

◇◇◇

Beyond the Afterlife & Back

Chapter 13

Opalescent Orbs

Sometimes, behind the curtain, amazing things await.

The third time I was taken back, I was roused from a deep sleep and was once again hurtling through space. Once again, Frank and Amos, my ever-present guides, met me as I left my body and accompanied me.

Each time, it required nothing on my part. Perhaps at some deep level, my higher-self was aware of it ahead of time, but my mortal mind knew nothing about it until I left my sleeping body. It was as if an undeniable force inextricably drew me to a destination beyond this world and my mortal mind had nothing to say about it before or at the time.

From then on, on the way over, I was just along for the ride, so to speak. But, it was entirely different coming back. As I have already mentioned, coming back to the exact time and place, wasn't so simple, and I didn't always get it right. So Frank and Amos saw to it that I got plenty of practice.

On the way over, Frank and Amos alluded to the fact that this trip to the afterlife was to be entirely different than the other two times. This time, they took me to a gathering of our old soul group, which we had all reincarnated with, over and over, for millennia.hyd.'

On this trip, there were no physical bodies again. I guess Frank and Amos felt I was becoming comfortable enough, to let go of the need for a physical appearance. I found later that sometimes, some part of my higher self would roll out a proper physical reality for me, I suppose for nostalgic reasons if nothing else. They were always fun and entertaining. Maybe, it was the past-lives spent in Tibet or Ireland, but for some reason, lush green meadows or majestic mountain vistas were some of my favorite forms of projections.

When I mentioned that, Frank ribbed me, reminding me, with amusement, that I sure was having trouble letting go of judgment. "What do you mean," I asked him, "how is that a judgment?"

He surprised me when he said, "Any comparison that makes something less or more, than something else, is a form of judgment and where we were going, I might want to be aware of that."

On this occasion, all the "entities" from our soul group, were in the form of opalescent orbs consisting of love and energy. Again, part of them I had known in this material universe, and the rest were from other realities in God's realm.

We were off in a quiet corner of the cosmos in a dark night sky, as thousands of these opalescent orbs wheeled and turned in space. They were all synchronously interacting in one large group, groups reminiscent of the vast flocks of birds or schools of fish as they wheeled and turned as a unit in the air or water, just as they had on the National Geographic Channel. However, these entities, in the form of beautiful opalescent orbs, were the essence of pure souls, expressing their endless love and bliss.

It was a joyous occasion. All communication was instantaneous from one immortal mind to another, each with perfect understanding in a form of communication akin to mental telepathy, but crystal clear and perfect. All thoughts were their original form. There was no filtering or censoring, just pure, nonjudgmental communication with the God part of us raidaiting everywhere. It was a jubilant reunion of souls, reminiscing about past times together, woven into coming adventures we were planning together.

All the shining orbs, together, composed a large shimmering globe, radiating love and happiness. I could look back in one direction and see a similar large shimmering sphere, representing our past incarnation together. Beyond that, a slightly smaller sphere, representing an even earlier time together.

In the other direction, a large shimmering globe represented our incarnation we were now planning. In either direction, like a beautiful string of pearls, our past, and future lives spread out into eternity. And we were experiencing the present between the past and future, in the eternal now.

It seemed that we were all looking back over past incarnations, just reminiscing and having fun as we decided on our futures. The interaction between two souls might go something like this:

"Boy, back in the 13th century in Italy, I really screwed up. Remember the time you ran in front of my horse and I whipped you for scaring the animals? Well, let's go down to earth and let me try it again, and maybe I'll get it right this time. Let's go to, say, Ashland, Oregon in the 21st century. I'll live on the corner of B Street and Eighth, and you can live anywhere in the area you decide. We'll meet some morning at the corner of C Street and Seventh as you pull out in front of my car, and we'll see if I get it right this time."

This gala of orbs was an incredible time of musing over our past times together in other times and places. As we reminisced, we were looking at times we could have made better choices. Then, taking the good and the bad together, we were planning other lives together, where we could try it over again, hoping that next time, we would get it right.

These Life Reviews covered all reincarnations, physical or nonphysical. This made sense when I later learned that a soul's progression is eternal. We will always be learning and growing, so there will always be reviews of old missteps and new plans for the future

To be notified when this book is available, go to duane@agnosticsNDE.org and you'll receive the free White Paper, *"The 6 Things You Didn't Know about NDEs"*

About the Author

As a young family man who was a non-believer in anything spiritual, he seemed to have it all; a beautiful home, a loving family, cars, boats, and airplanes. He seemingly had everything money could buy, at least until a Doctor from Stanford Medical Center told him he had only five months to live.

However, as an agnostic he had no fear of death, expecting only oblivion when he died. Instead, he encountered a surprising Near Death Experience, or in his case, an After Death Experience. Then, as with many other Death Survivors, he too, was sent back to tell his story. To tell people that death is nothing to fear, in fact, it is quite the opposite.

Then, following his original death and return to this life, he was returned to the Afterlife on five separate occasions. On these ensuing trips, as he left his body he was met by his Soul Guides, Frank, and Amos, and they began a 30-year preparation for what he was being sent back to do. Finally, after 25 years of instruction and learning, Frank and Amos finally told him it was time to write. With plenty of help from his two Soul Guides, they have finished six books. The two first books were on educational theory, as he was taught how to write from the Inner Voice. The other four were concerning his experiences with the Afterlife and, Frank and Amos.

Now, in early 2015, they are telling him it is time to publish his first volume, *Dying to Really Live.* It's the story of what led to his original After Death Experience and death was like. In addition, it is about what he saw, learned and did in the Afterlife, and how it felt to return to this life after experiencing what he did.

The other three books are about his other trips to the Afterlife, as well as the 33-years it took Frank and Amos to prepare him for what he was sent back to do. They will be published, one a month, following this first book of the NDE Series.

These books speak to the most exciting time in all of Earth's history. It is about finding our Soul's true purpose and the role for which God created them; a unique role which only they can fulfill in this, the final unfolding of His perfect plan for the Material Universe.

To be notified when the author's next book in the series is available, go to www.NDEsurvivor.org and receive a free White Paper, *The 6 Things You Didn't Know About NDEs.*"

CPSIA information can be obtained
at www.ICGtesting.com
Printed in the USA
LVHW04s1528240818
587634LV00001B/105/P